ART DEVOTIONALS

Cute and simple drawings inspired by Scripture

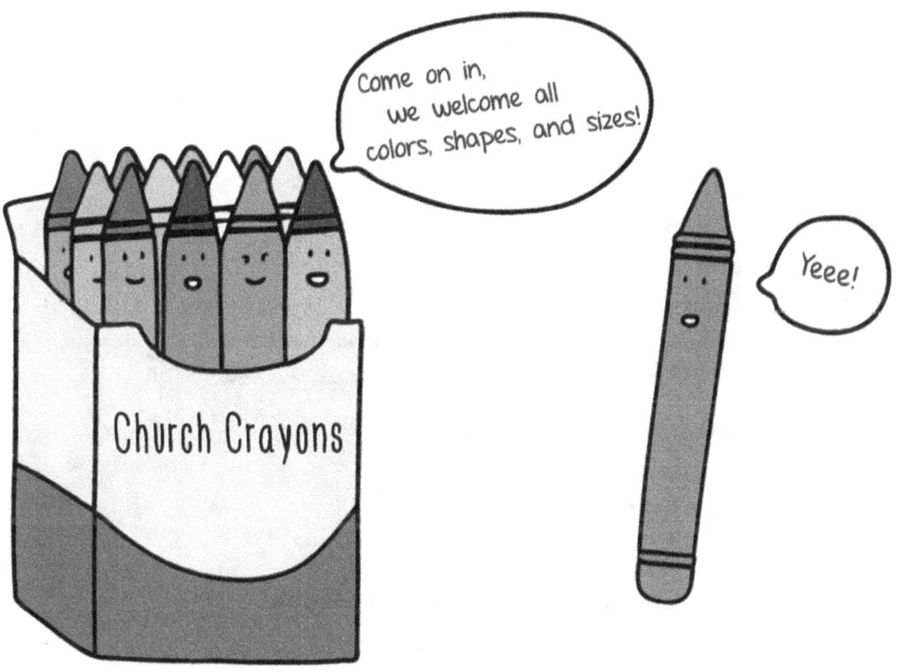

With application and journal pages on the back!

By Nuo Liu

"Let all that I am praise the Lord;
May I never forget the good things He does for me"

Psalm 103:2

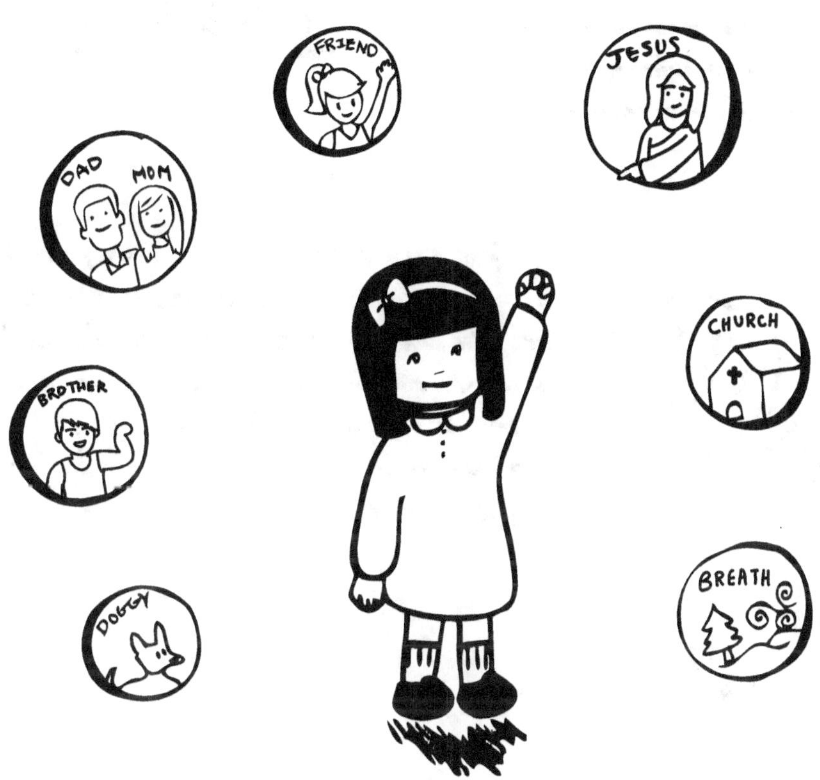

I started drawing daily devotionals because for a while I lost sight of who God was and all His blessings. So everyday I would meditate on a verse, and when an image came to my mind I would draw it right into my sketchbook. It was a personal way for me to remember God's word and apply it to my life. I hope these drawings bring joy to your life and remind you of the amazing love God has for you!

– Nuo

Guide to this book

The drawings in this book are based on my interpretations of Scripture. To understand the true meaning of each verse, please take time to look up the verse in the bible and really read it in context. Even better with a friend or family member!

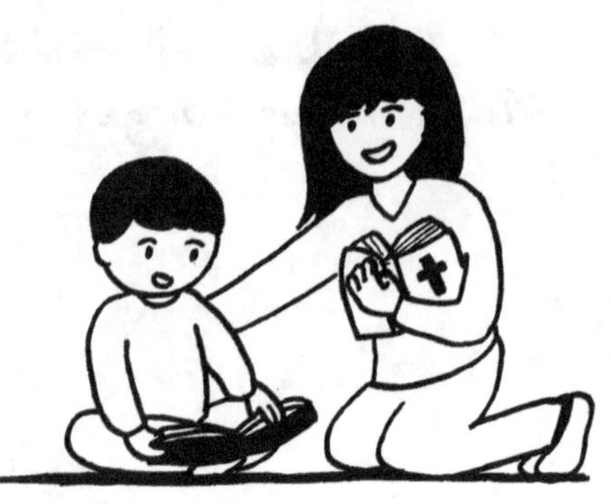

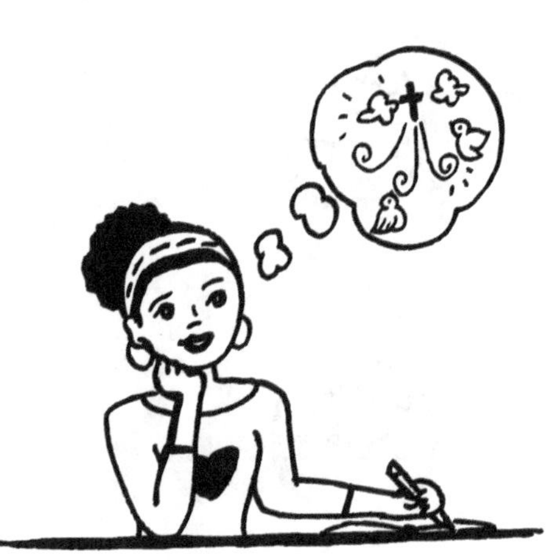

This book is interactive, so feel free to color, doodle, or write in it! Each page on the back includes a devotional and room for you to put down your thoughts. Fill it up with drawings or words that God has put on your heart.

Whenever you see this figure, it is supposed to represent Jesus or God. It just happens to be how I think He looks like. For God is Spirit, and though we may all see Him differently, His character still remains the same!

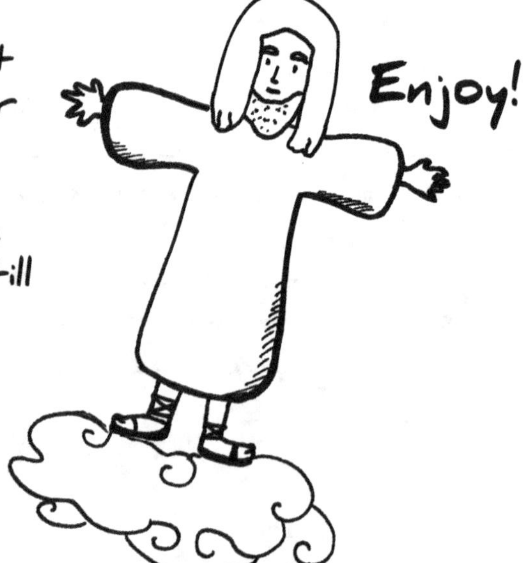

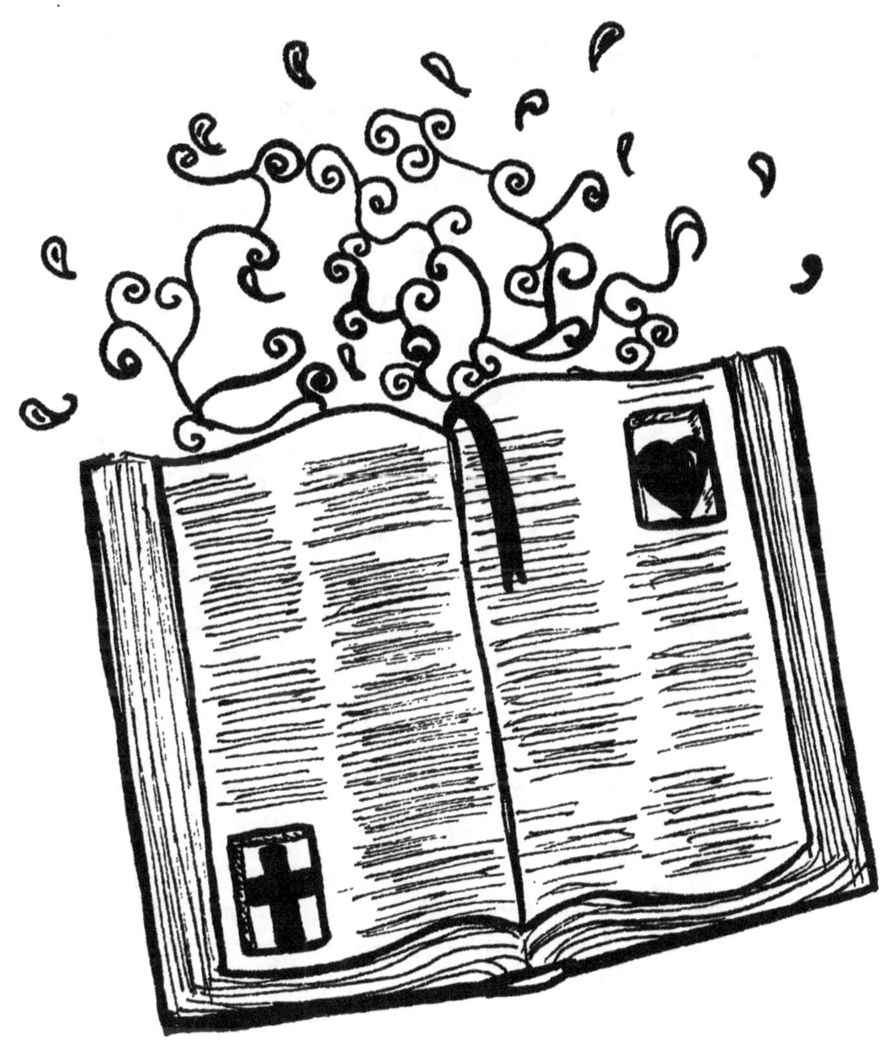

"All Scripture is breathed out by God and profitable for teaching, for reproof, for correction, and for training in righteousness"

2 Timothy 3:16

Reading Scripture is an excellent way for us to know God better and to know what our purpose is in life. Although not everything we read will seem fun and exciting, it is still important to have an understanding of it because it shapes the meaning of our faith. As we read, we have to pay close attention to what God is teaching us and then put it into practice.

How do you spend time reading God's word? What are ways you can apply what you read to your everyday life?

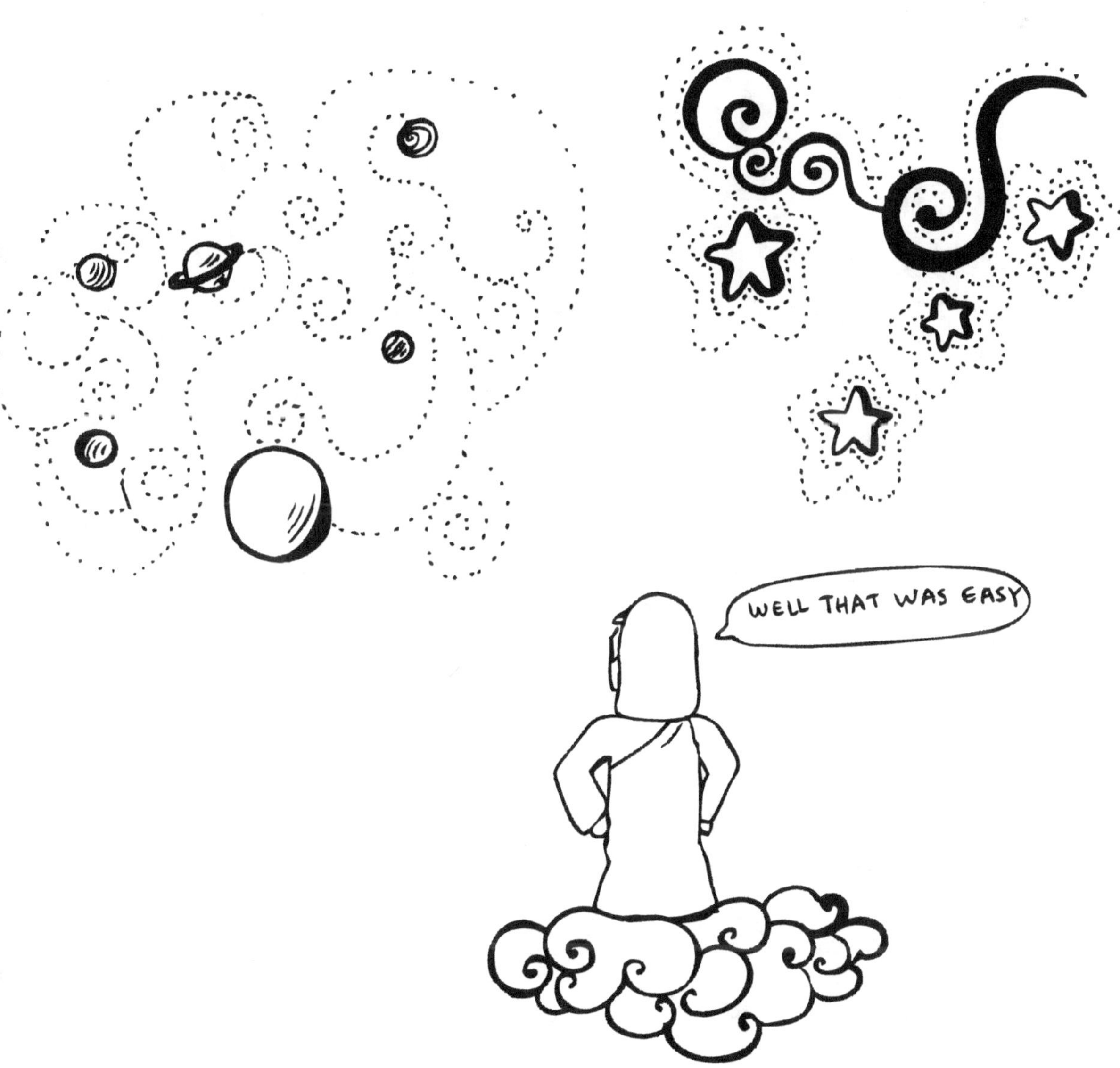

"In the beginning God created the heavens and the earth."

Genesis 1:1

God is so creative. He not only created the heavens and the earth, but He created you and me! As His creations, we have the ability to create things just as beautiful and magnificent.

Close your eyes for a minute and imagine what the creation of heaven and earth looks like to you. When you open your eyes, draw or write down the image you see in the space below.

Flood Survivors

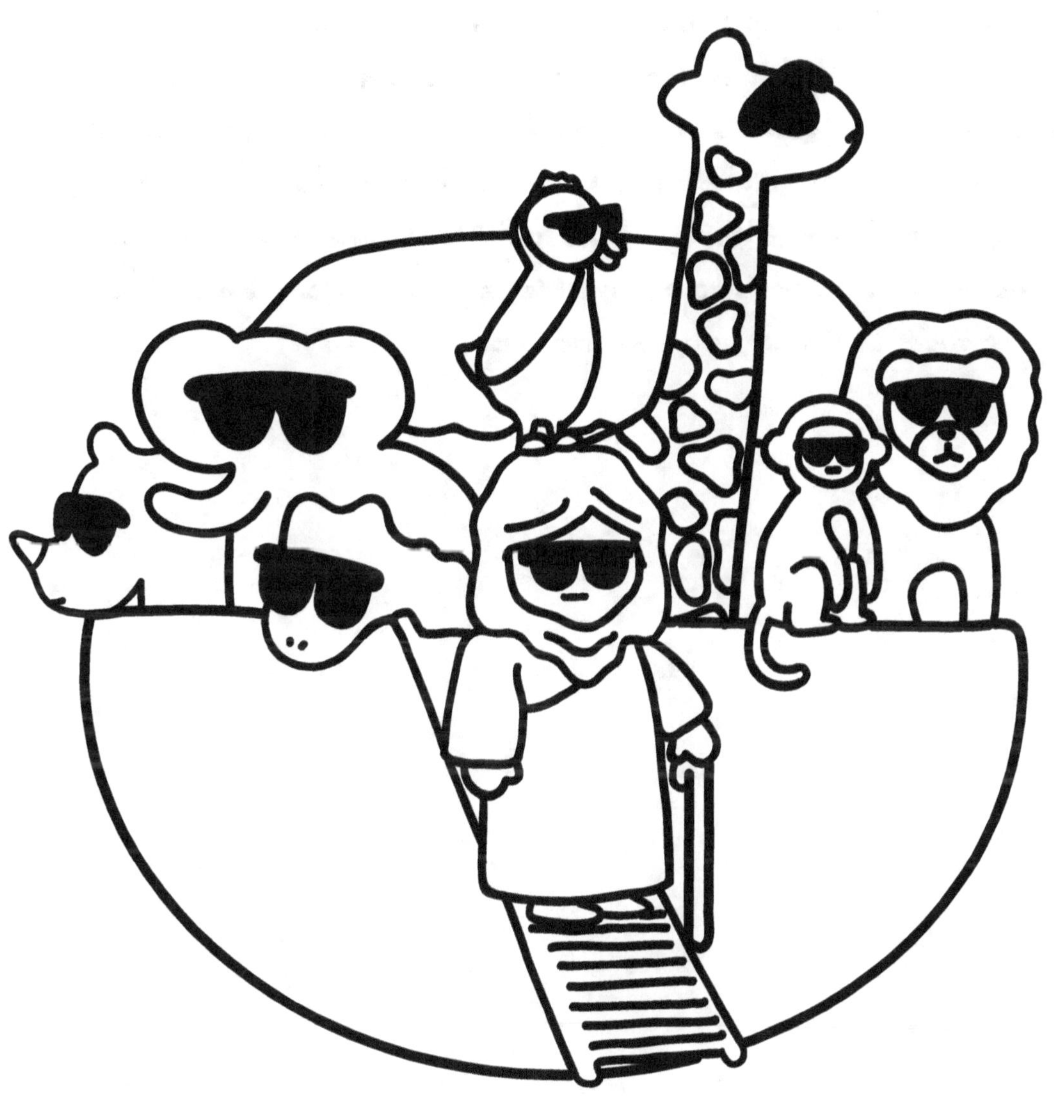

God gave Noah a very big task of building an ark that will hold two of every animal. This seems like a crazy thing to do, but Noah obeyed God and did exactly what he was told. As a result, Noah and his family survived through the biggest flood on earth! He is a survivor because he trusted God every step of the way.

There may be a time God is telling you to do something but fear stops you from doing it. Are you afraid of what others might think or say? Or do you doubt your ability? Look at the example of Noah and how he did not let fear or doubt stop him. He is a survivor, and if you put your trust in God, you can be too!

"With what can we compare the kingdom of God, or what parable shall we use for it? It is like a grain of mustard seed, which, when sown on the ground, is the smallest of all the seeds on earth,
yet when it is sown it grows up and becomes larger than all the garden plants and puts out large branches, so that the birds of the air can make nests in its shade."

Mark 4:30-32

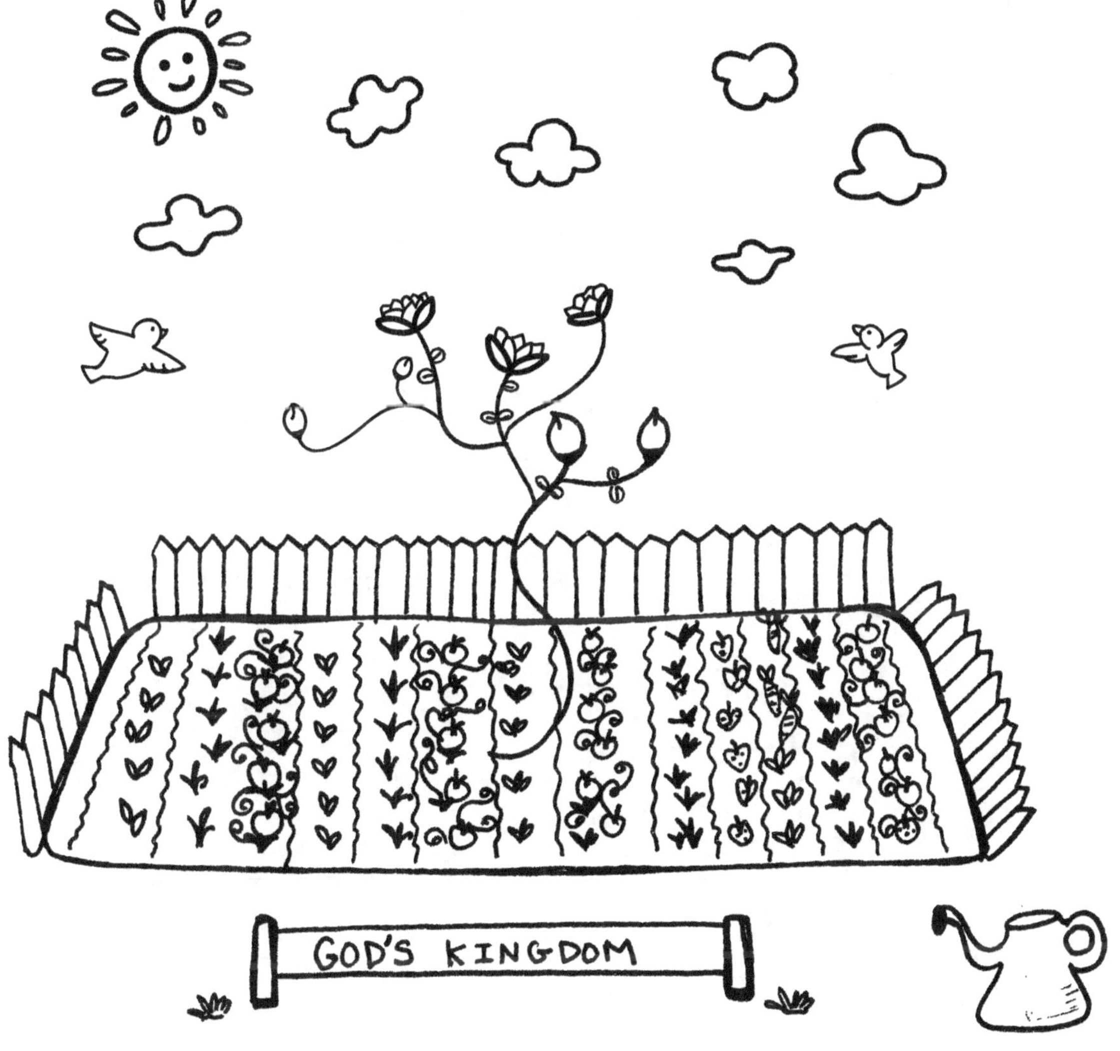

 Jesus describes God's kingdom as a small seed that grows into a beautiful garden. Our lives are a part of this wonderful design and each of us play a very important role. Keep watering yourself with God's word and His spirit because He will use you to plant seeds across the world. One day you will see this beautiful garden and know that you were a part of its generation!

 How would you describe or illustrate God's kingdom? What do you think is your role in His kingdom?

I will praise You in the morning

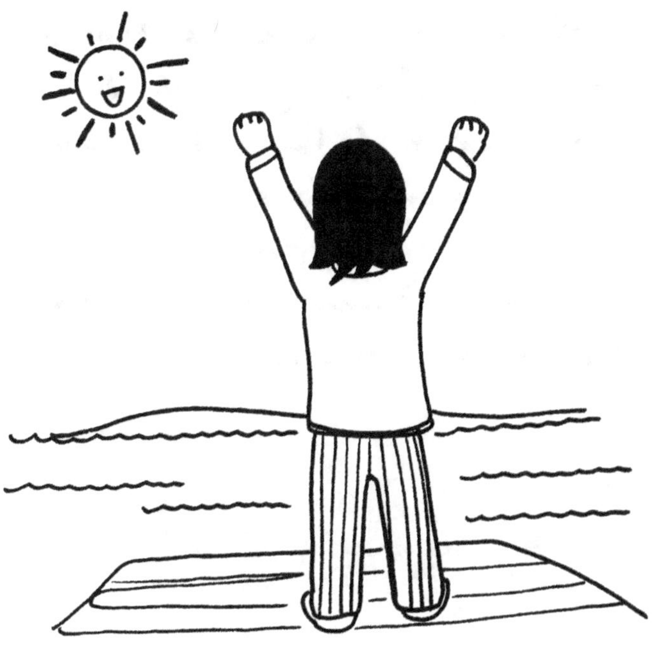

I will praise You in the evening

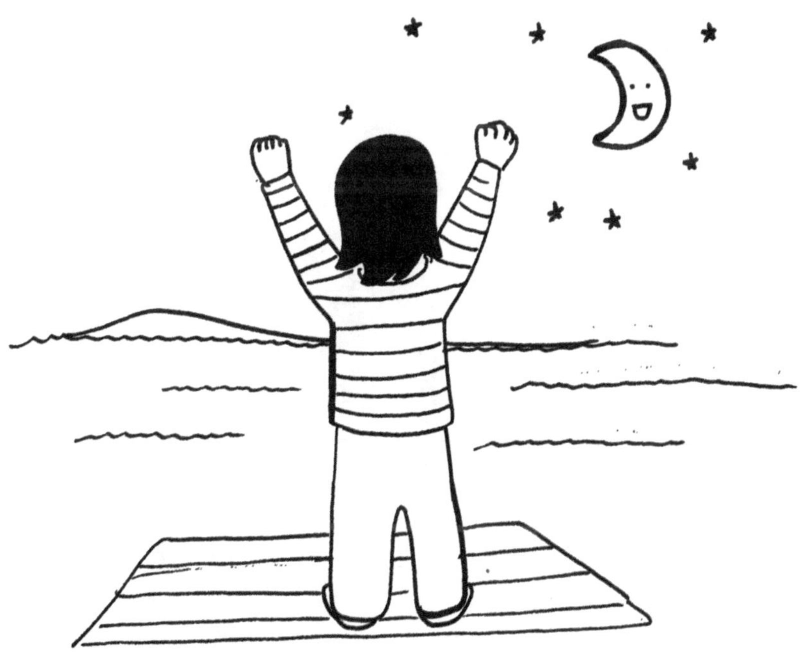

ALL DAY EVERY DAY!

To praise God means to give thanks to Him. God loves it when we praise Him and He has given us more than enough to be thankful for. We can praise Him through many different ways, whether it's through song, dance, or even a thought. This is the freedom He has given us and we should be praising Him all throughout the day!

Think of ten things you can praise God for today and write or draw them down. Spend some time right now to praise Him for these things however He has created you to!

"If God is for us, who can be against us?"

Romans 8:31

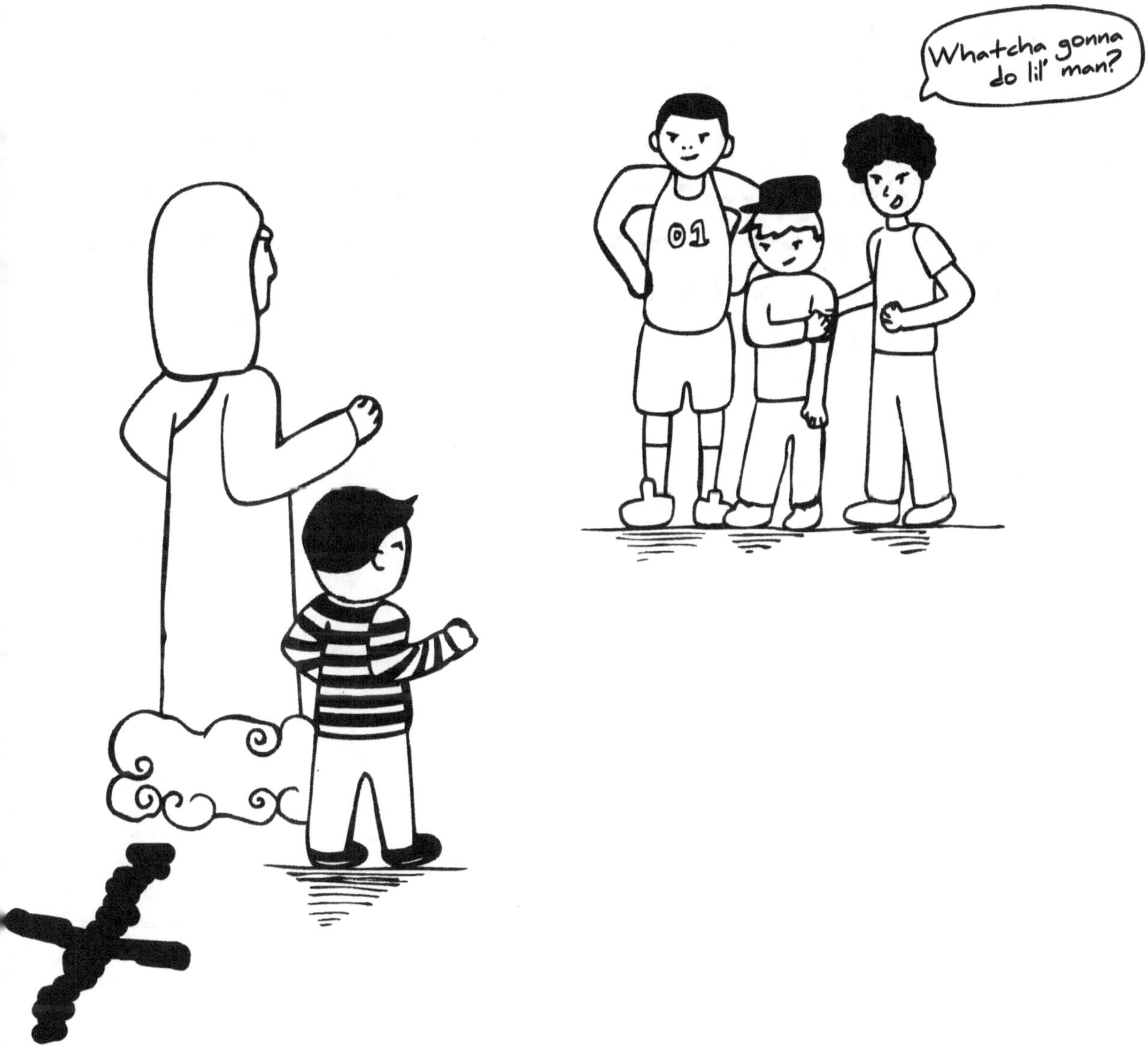

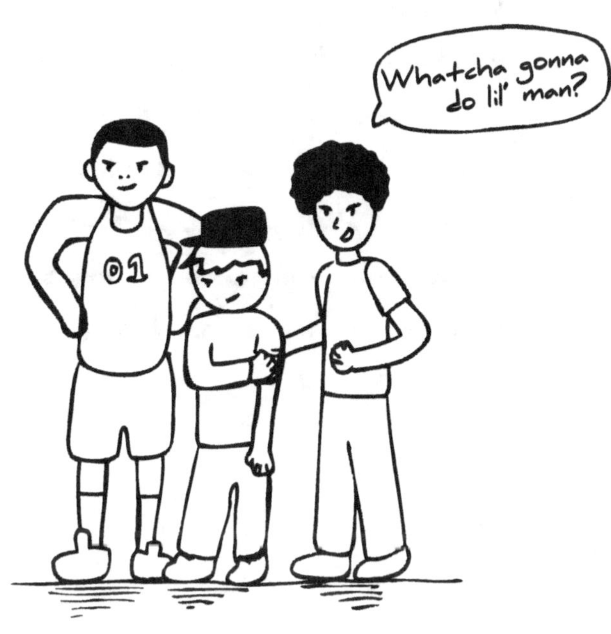

Standing up for what you believe in can be a scary thing when you feel like you have no support. You may think you are alone, but the great news is that you have an almighty God who is right by your side! When we feel weak and don't know what to do, we must call on Him for strength and guidance. God has conquered it all, so through Him we can be conquerors too!

Have you ever faced a situation where you had to stand up for your beliefs? Did you trust completely in God or did you hold back? List the strengths of God below and remember these strengths the next time you face a similar situation.

"I am the bread of life; whoever comes to me shall not hunger, and whoever believes in me shall never thirst."

John 6:35

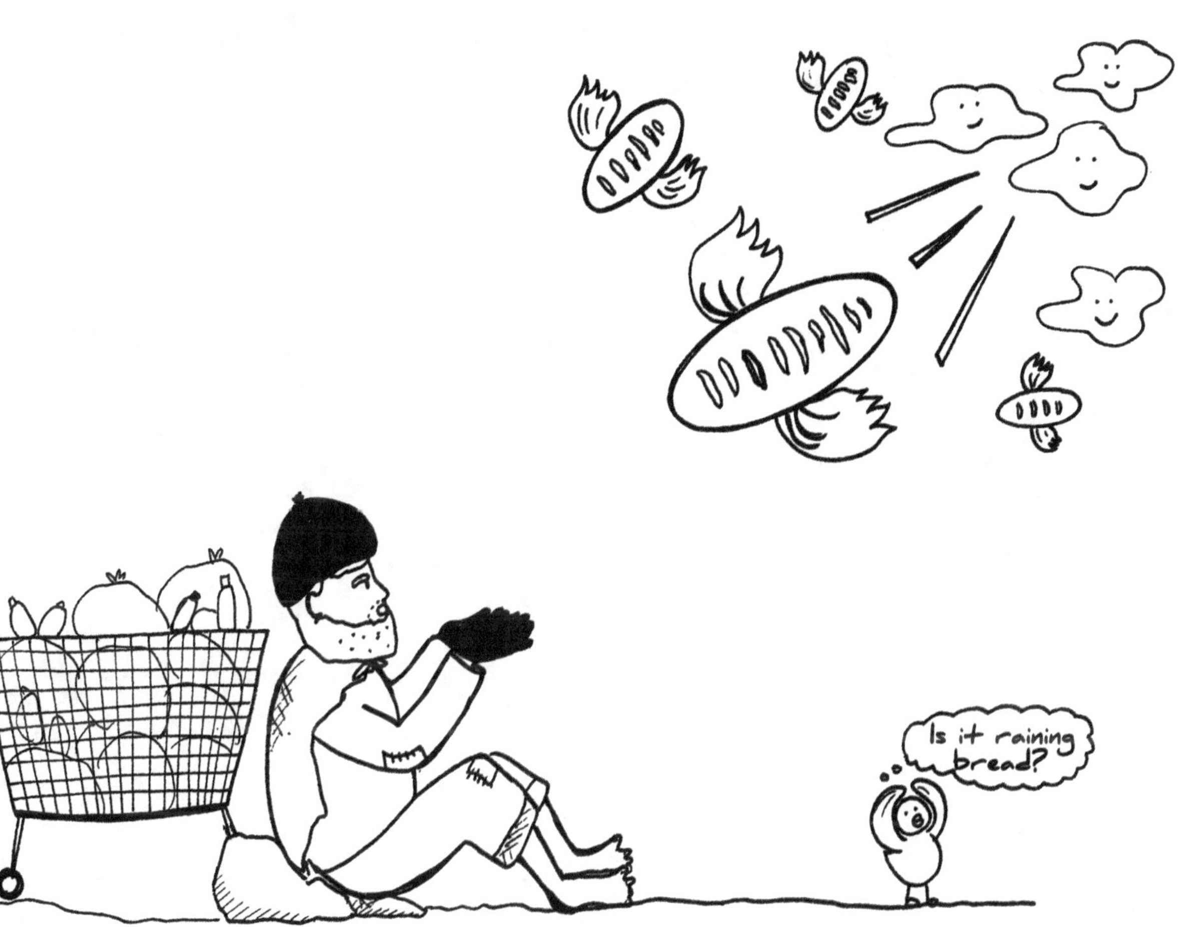

We all need food in order to survive. But just as we need to nourish our body with food, we need to nourish our soul as well. The only food that will satisfy our soul comes from God in heaven. God has given us Jesus who is our bread of life, and if we let Him nourish us, we will be full and satisfied everyday.

Have you had a taste of this bread of life? How can you share this bread of life with others?

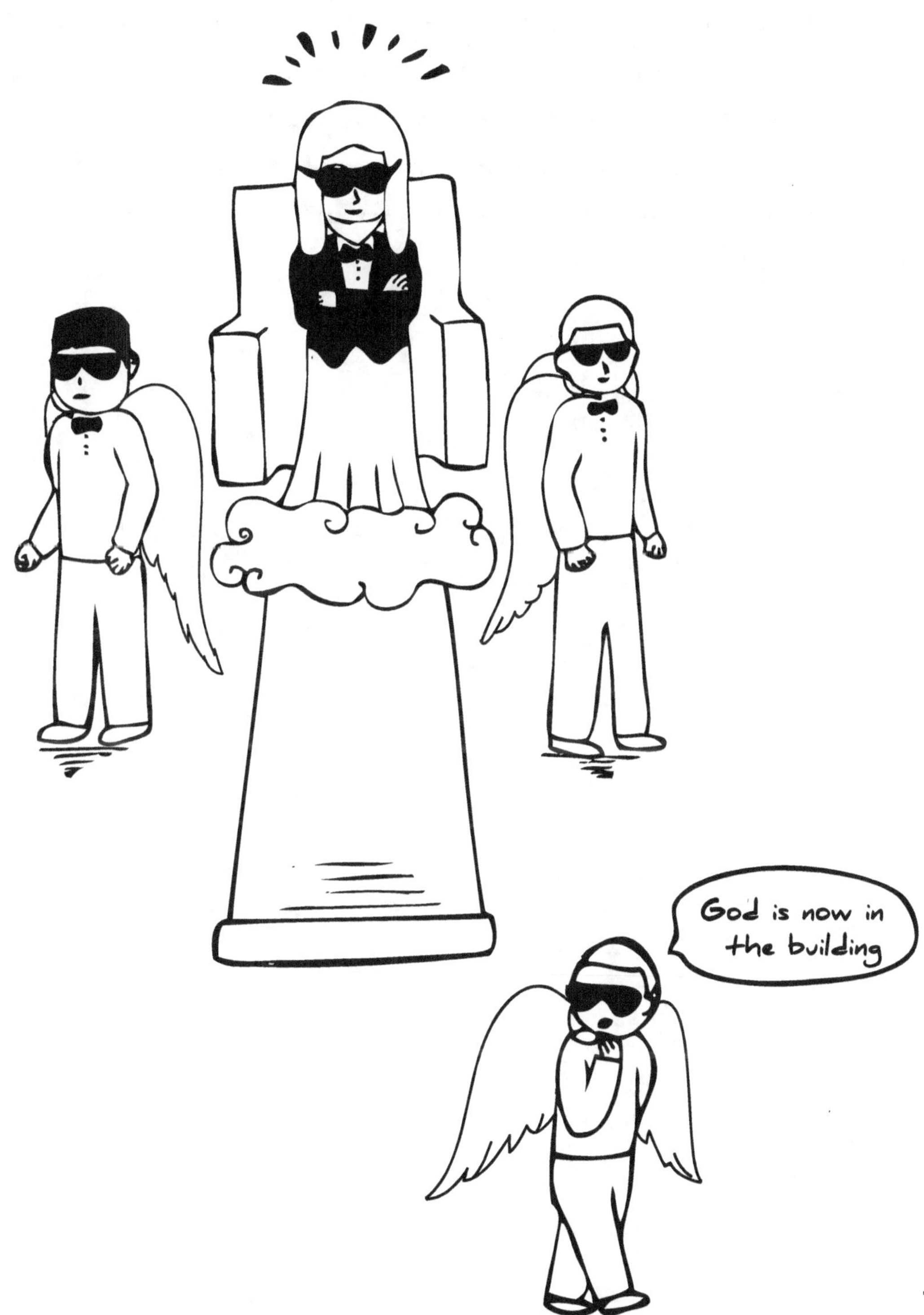

"Holy, holy, holy is the Lord Almighty;
the whole earth is full of his glory."
Isaiah 6:3 (NIV)
God is now in the building

God is the most powerful and almighty figure on this earth. No celebrity can even compare to the greatness of God. But regardless of His status, He still chooses to be by our side, walking with us through life on earth. Lets not forget He is with us at all times and to not steal His spotlight! God wants us to be made known, but He wants us to be known for Him and His glory.

Do you give God the respect He deserves? What are some ways you can give attention to Him instead of yourself?

"All we like sheep have gone astray;
we have turned—every one—to his own way;
and the Lord has laid on him
the iniquity of us all."
Isaiah 53:6
Hold on Chop Chop,
I got you!
- Baahelp!

Just like Chop Chop, all of us were once heading down the wrong path. But like a good shepherd, Jesus watches out for each of us and guides us back to where we belong. Even in our wandering and mistakes, He still risked His life for us so that we can be safe and secure.

Have you ever found yourself going down a dangerous path? If you know God is your good shepherd, what path is He guiding you to? Draw a picture of these two paths below and the things that can lead to these paths.

"For this son of mine was dead and has come to life again; he was lost and has been found."
And they began to celebrate.

Luke 15:24

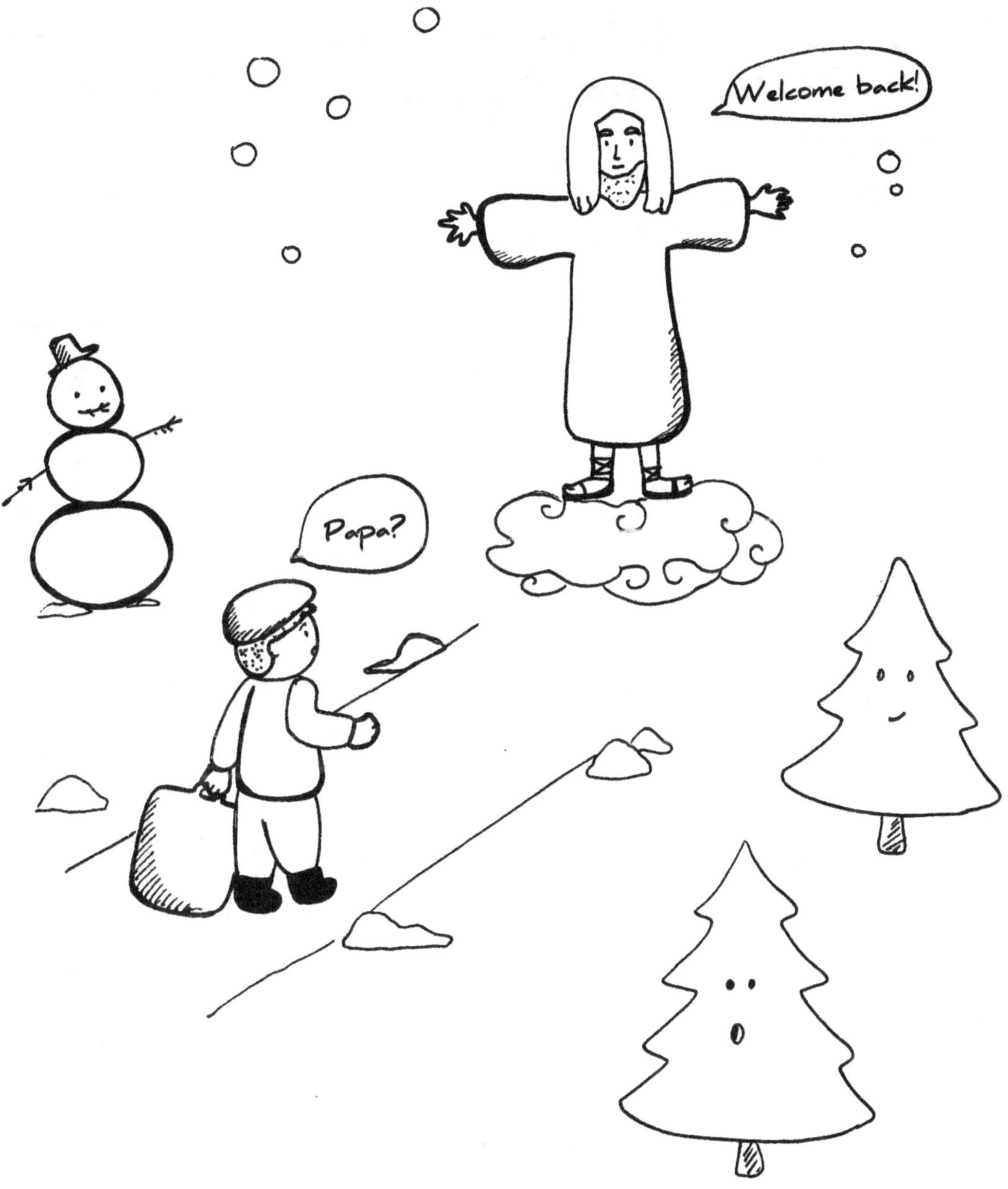

God loves each and every one of us. Even when we stray away, He will search for us and welcome us back with open arms. Do not ever think your sins are too bad for God to love you! He loves us the same no matter who we are or what we have done.

Take some time now to enjoy being in the arms of God. Because you are united with Him and nothing can separate you from His love, think of ways you can celebrate this great news!

"This is the day that the Lord has made;
let us rejoice and be glad in it."

Psalm 118:24

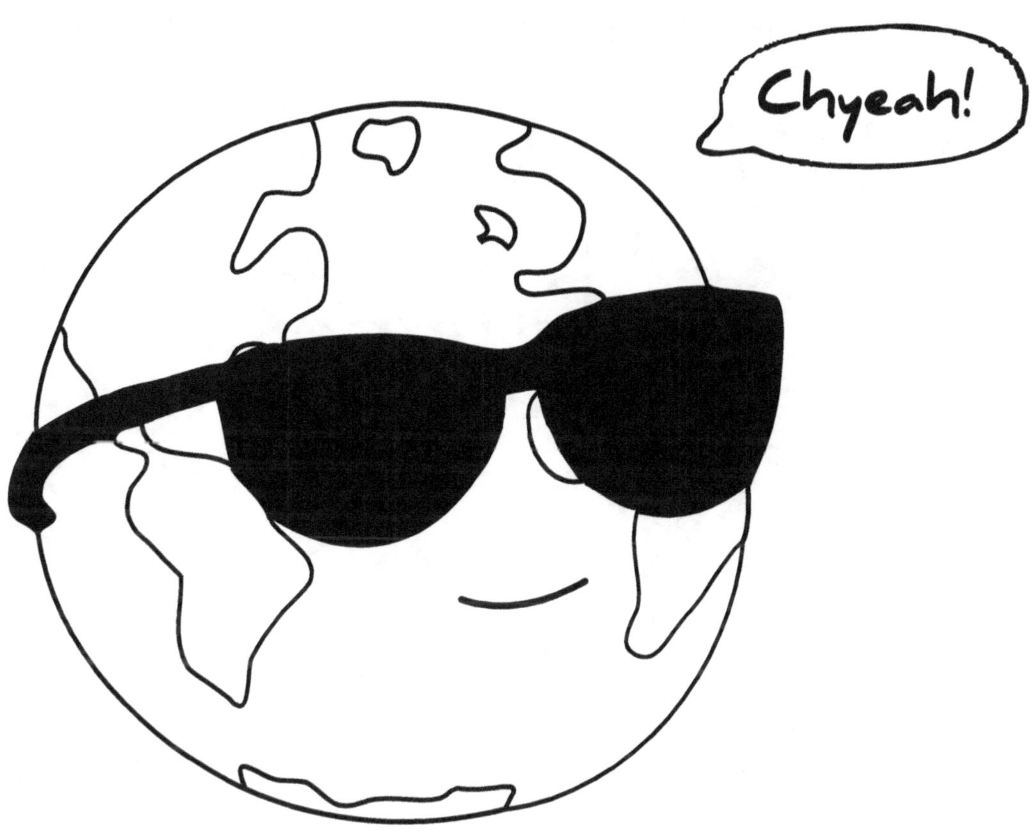

God woke you up today for a purpose. Whether today is filled with something new and exciting or it's something you've always been doing, do everything with a positive attitude and a cheerful heart. Thank God for giving you another day and pray that your thoughts, words, and actions will give Him the most glory!

Are you excited for today? If so, what are some words or phrases you can say to express how you feel?

"That is why, for Christ's sake, I delight in weaknesses, in insults, in hardships, in persecutions, in difficulties. For when I am weak, then I am strong."

2 Corinthians 12:10 (NIV)

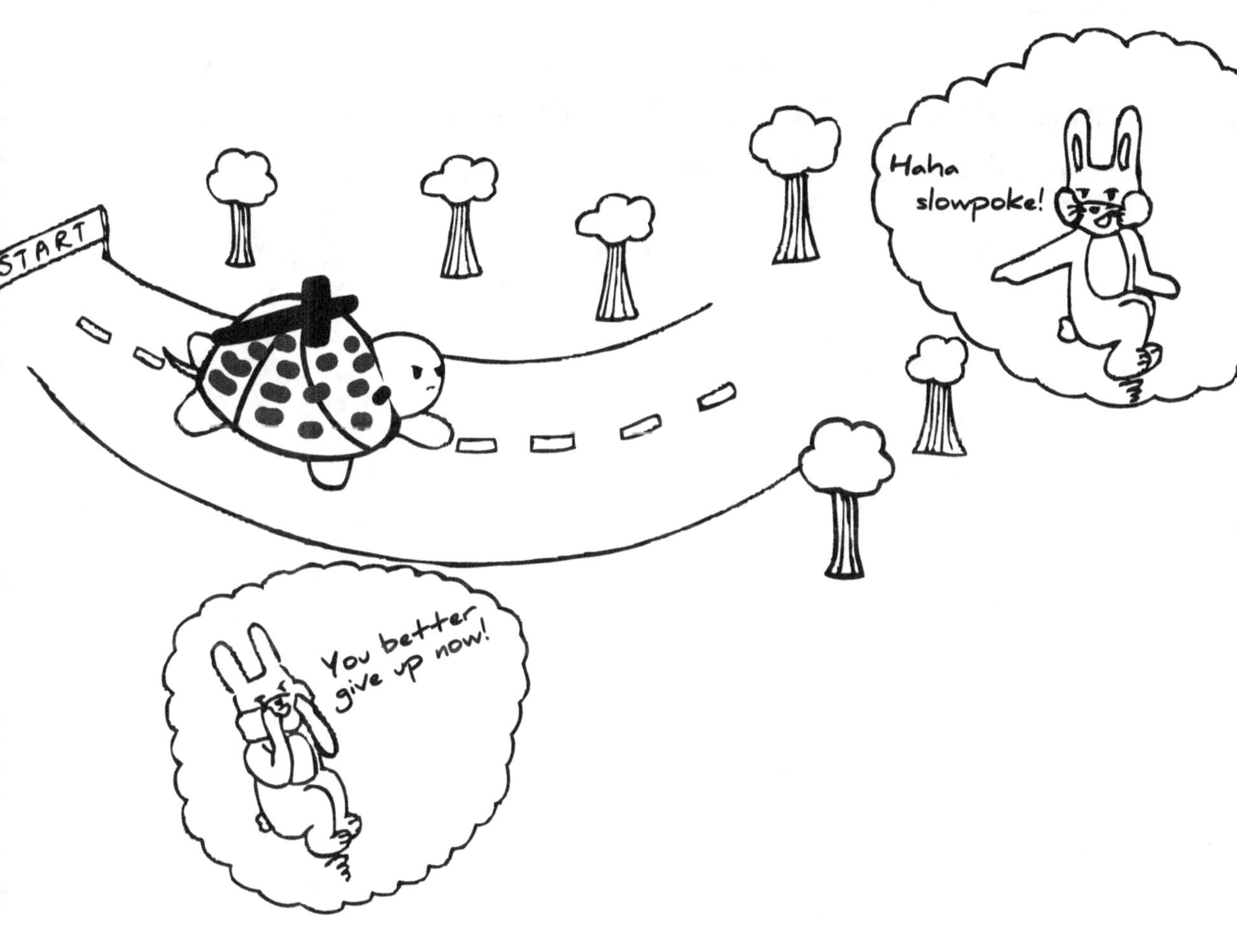

When we are living for God, things won't always be easy from start to finish. Sometimes we will run into thoughts, situations, or words from others that will make us feel like we are not good enough. Don't ever let those voices stop you from going! The most important voice we need to focus on is God's, and by putting our trust in Him, He will give us the power and confidence we need to cross the finish line.

Have you ever gone through something that was really difficult? What did you do? What can you find as your motivation to push through difficult times?

Senior Class of 28 A.D.

Delilah

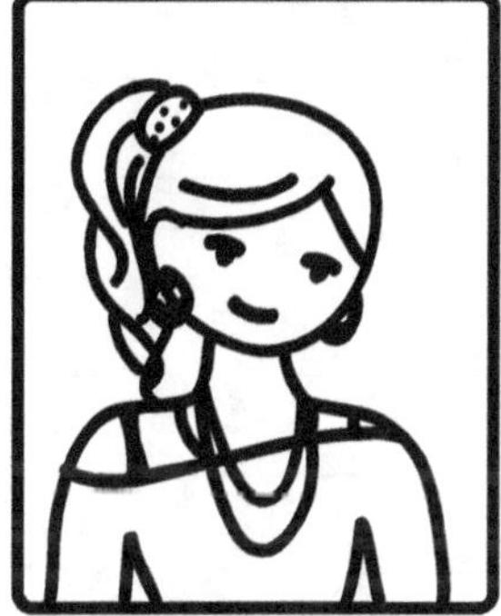

"Biggest Flirt"

Jesus Christ

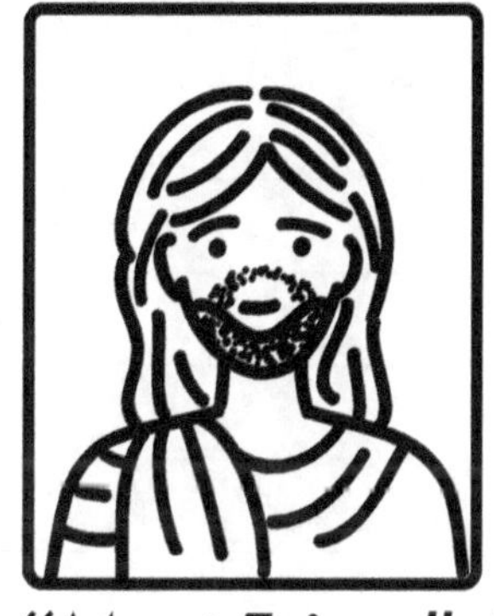

"Most Friendly"
"Most Reliable"
"Best Leadership"
"Most likely to live forever"
"Best Hair"

David

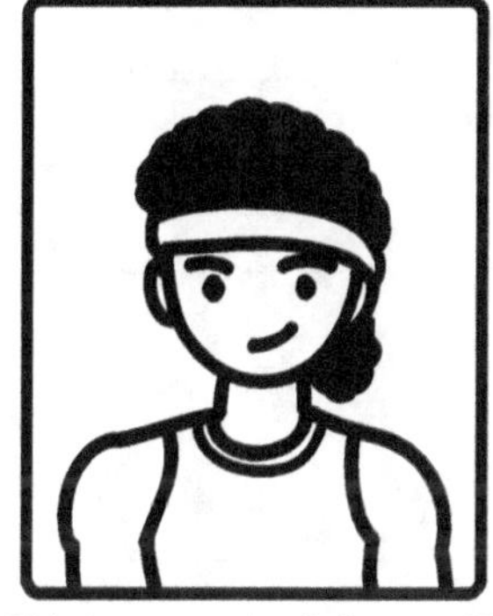

"Most Athletic"

Paul

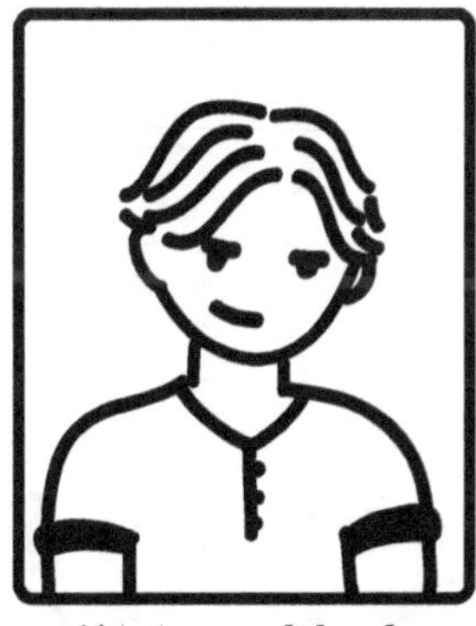

*"Most likely
to go to prison"*

John

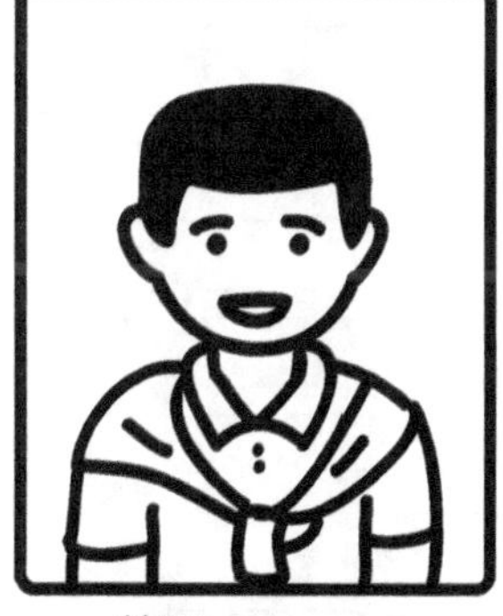

*"Biggest
Teacher's Pet"*

Esther

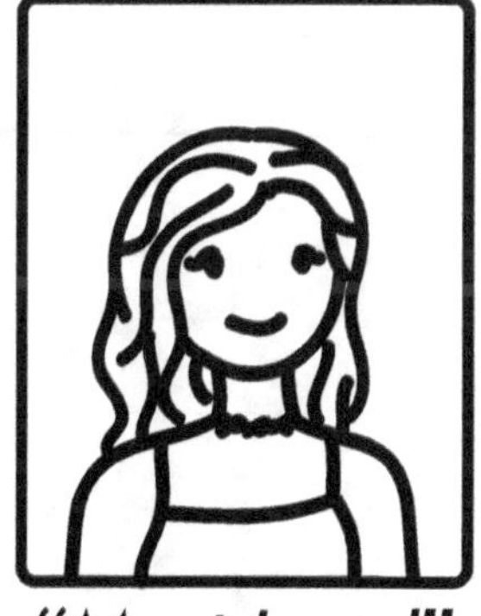

"Most Loyal"

Jesus can be known for many things. He can be a loving father, a best friend, a wise couselor, and the list goes on. Even though He has so many roles, He still makes time for me and you. This means we can go to Him for just about anything at anytime. What a friend we have in Jesus!

What other roles does Jesus play in your life?

Escalator to Heaven

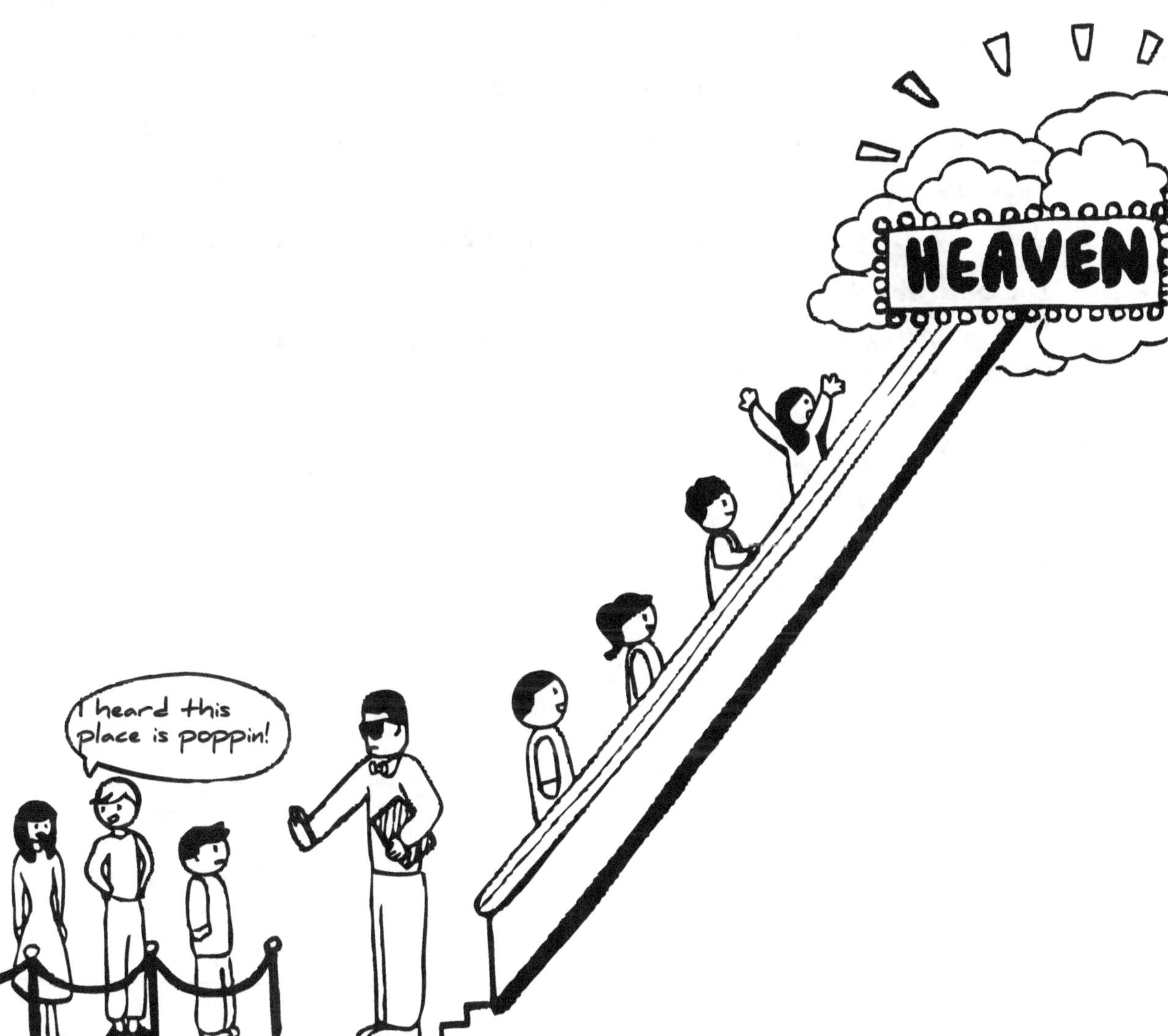

Imagine entering a big amusement park that has everything you've ever dreamed of. A place where you can go on as many rides as you want and never get sick. That's what heaven is going to be like. But because everyone wants to get in, not everyone will enter. Jesus says, "only those who actually do the will of my Father in heaven will enter" (Matthew 7:21). This means not only do we have to believe in Jesus in our hearts, but we have to follow what He says through our actions. If you surrender your life to Him this way, then you have a free ticket to the best place beyond earth!

What do you imagine heaven to look like?

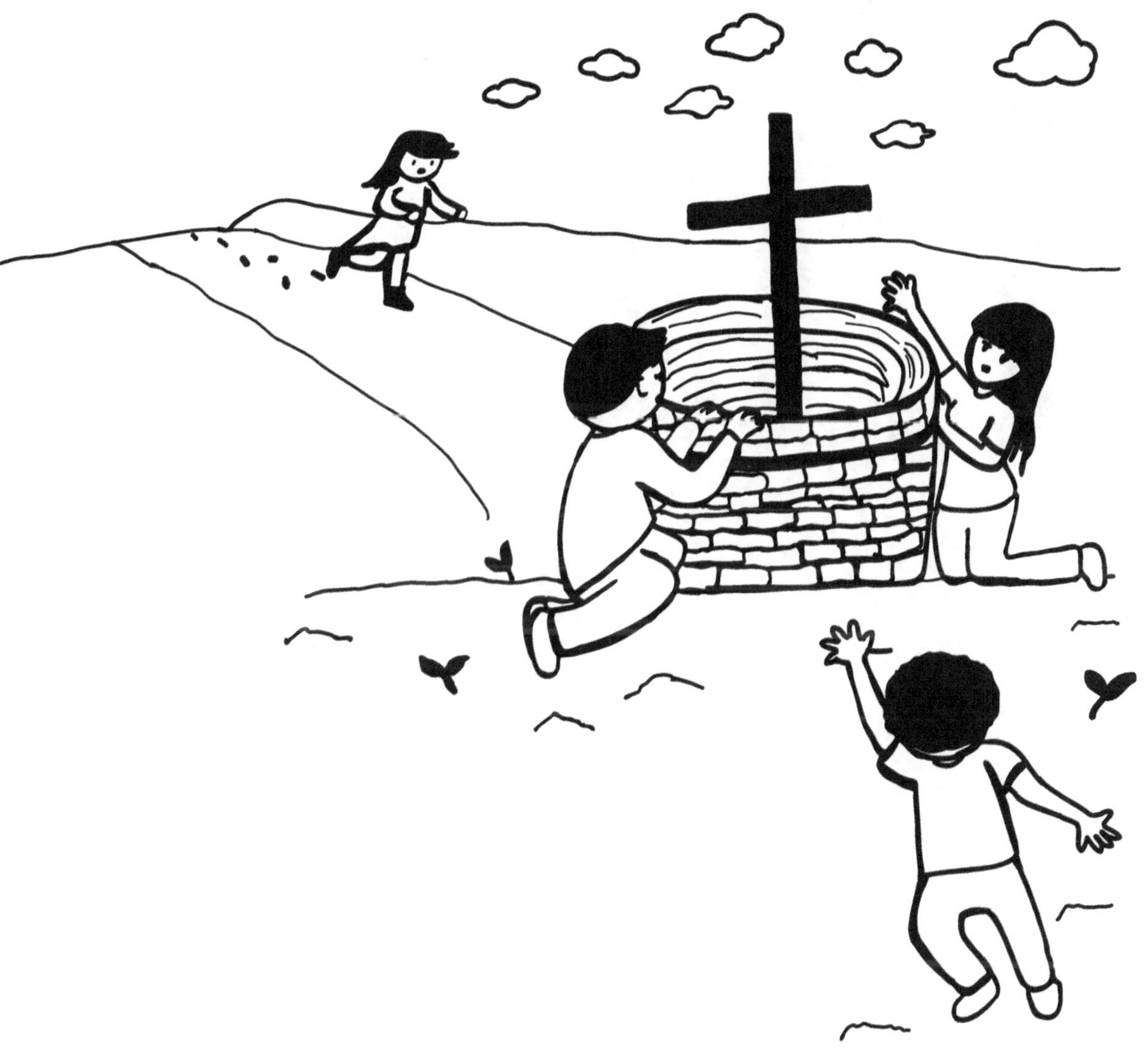

"Come to me, all who are weary and burdened, and I will give you rest"

Matthew 11:28 (NIV)

Jesus invites us to come to Him because He has something that we need. It's the cure that will give us a peace of mind and a restful soul. Before you turn to anything or anyone else, run to Him and tell Him your greatest need. He listens and He is commited to His promises. Keep running to Jesus and believe He will give you the peace and joy you desire!

Do you turn to Jesus first whenever you are in need of something? How do you go to Him?

"It is for freedom that Christ has set us free. Stand firm, then, and do not let yourselves be burdened again by a yoke of slavery."

Galatians 5:1 (NIV)

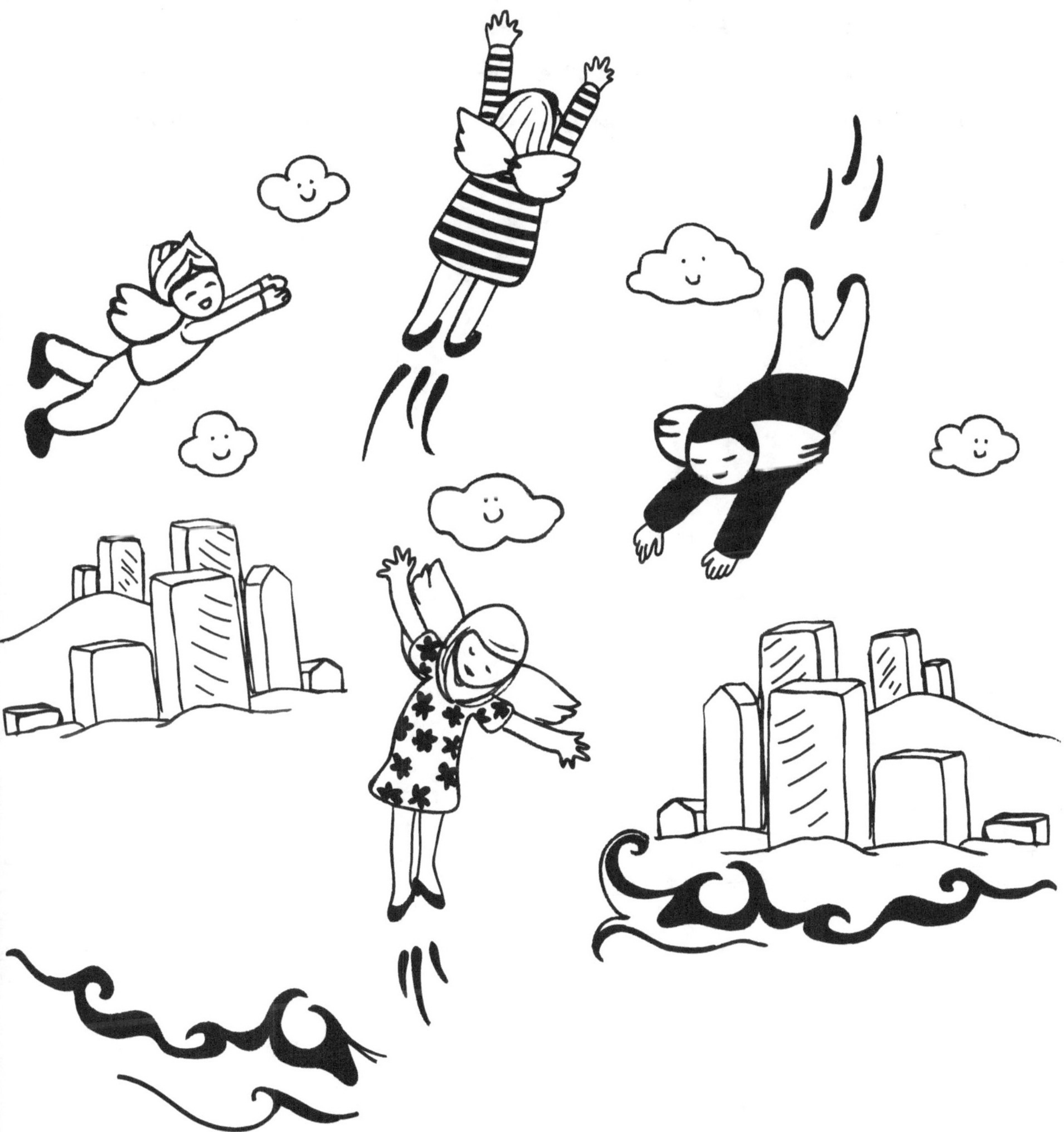

Jesus came to this earth so that our souls can be free from sin. But sometimes we forget about our freedom and we go back to feeling trapped. Stay strong and remember that Jesus fought and conquered sin, judgement, and death so that we can be free. Life may get hard at times, but one day in heaven we will all be completely worry free from the troubles of this earth.

What does it look like for you to be completely free? Is there anything holding you back from this freedom?

"The Lord is my shepherd, I shall not want. He makes me
lie down in green pastures;
He leads me beside quiet waters."

Psalms 23:1-2 (NASB)

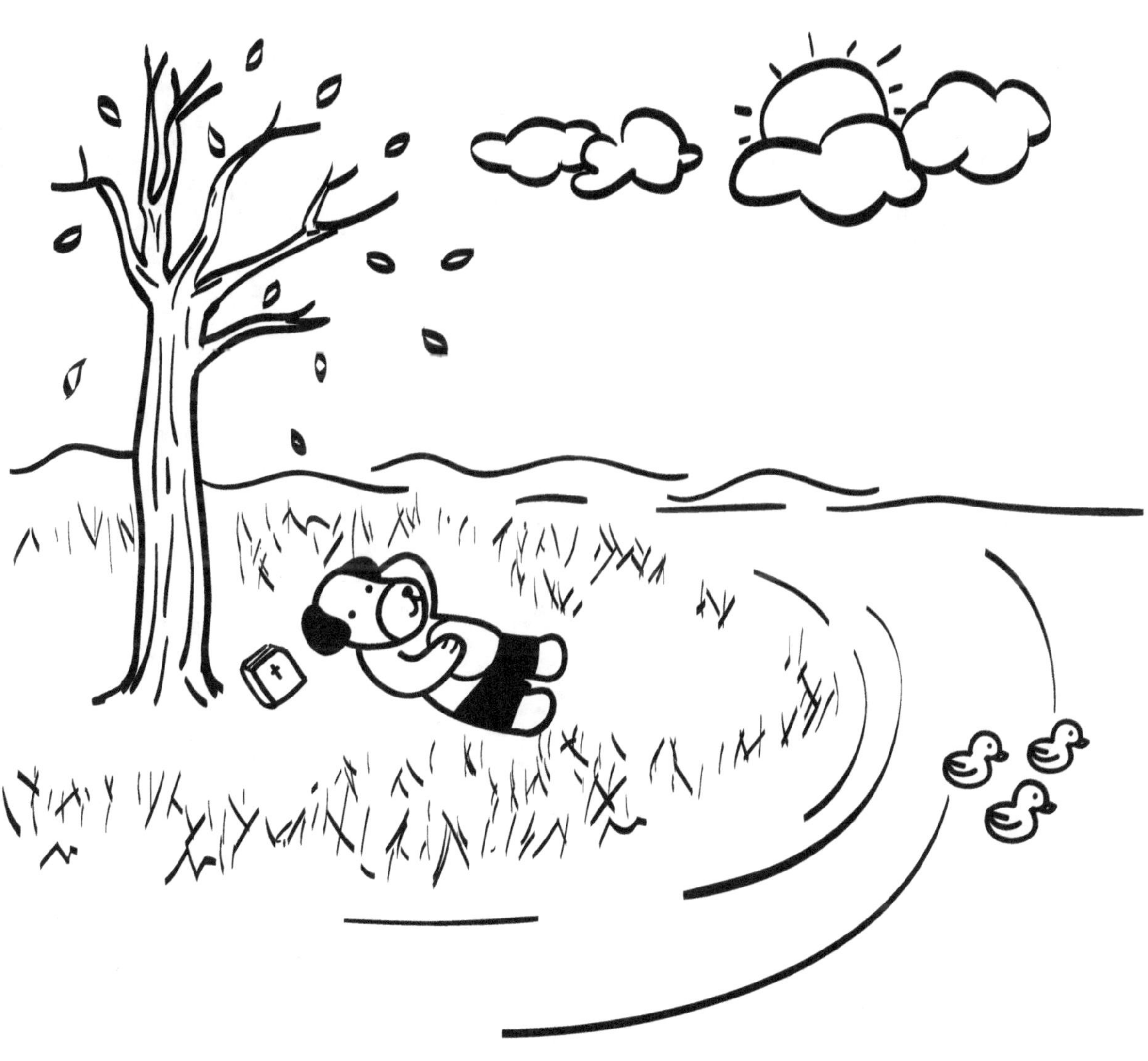

Having a relationship with God brings us to a place of peace and rest. If we spend more time with Him daily, He will bring us to that place no matter what trouble surrounds us.

Close your eyes and picture a place of peace with God and draw it below.

"But the fruit of the Spirit is love, joy, peace, patience, kindness, goodness, faithfulness, gentleness, self-control; against such things there is no law."

Galatians 5:22-23

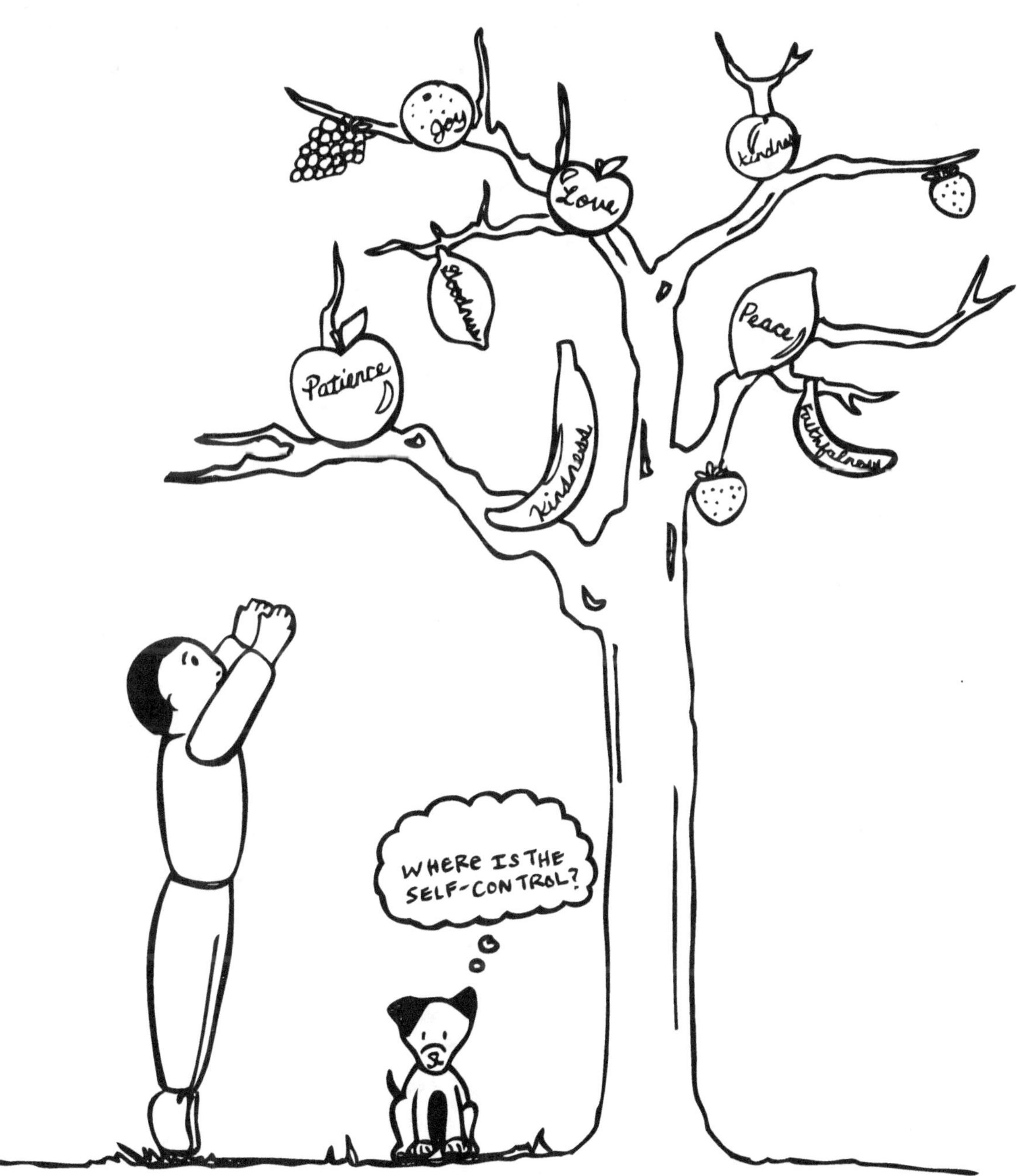

When we accept the Holy Spirit, we allow God to plant seeds of His character into our lives. These seeds will eventually become fruits of the Spirit, but we must be patient and allow God to work in us. As we turn to God daily, the bad fruit of our nature will rot away to make room for the good fruit of His nature.

What are some bad fruit you want to get rid of in your life and what are some good fruit you hope to produce?

"For God so loved the world that He gave his one and only Son, that whoever believes in Him shall not perish but have eternal life."

John 3:16 (NIV)

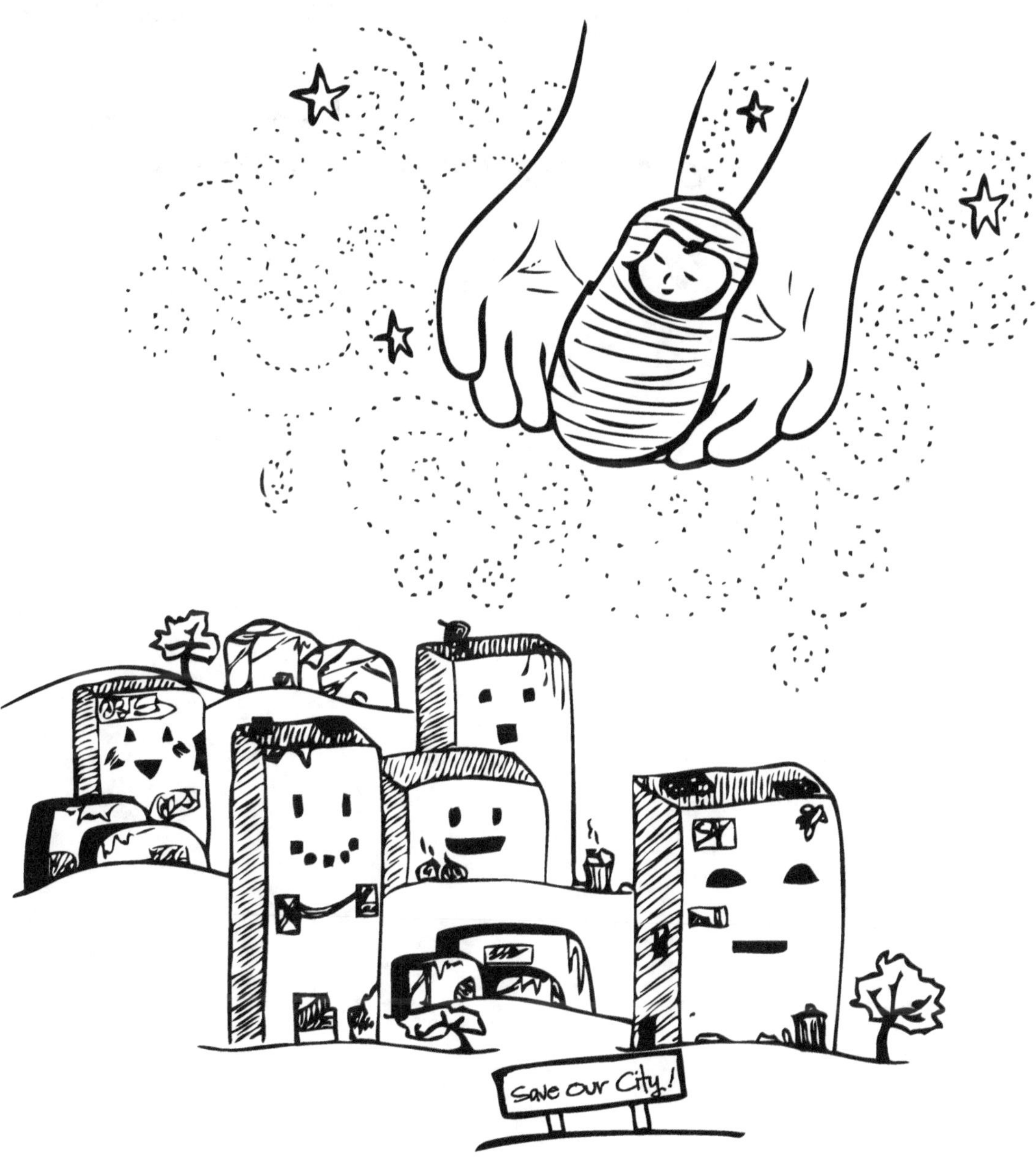

The greatest gift of love is when God gave His only son to a world that was in need of saving. He risked His life for us so that we can have a life filled with hope and a future. All of this was given not because we deserve it, but because God loves us. If you recognize that you are in need of saving, know that God is waiting for you to accept His gift. If you have already accepted Jesus in your life, use your life to share this gift to others.

Take time now to thank God for loving you. Pray about how you can give the gift of love to others.

"So whether you eat or drink, or whatever you do, do it all for the glory of God."

1 Corinthians 10:31 (NIV)

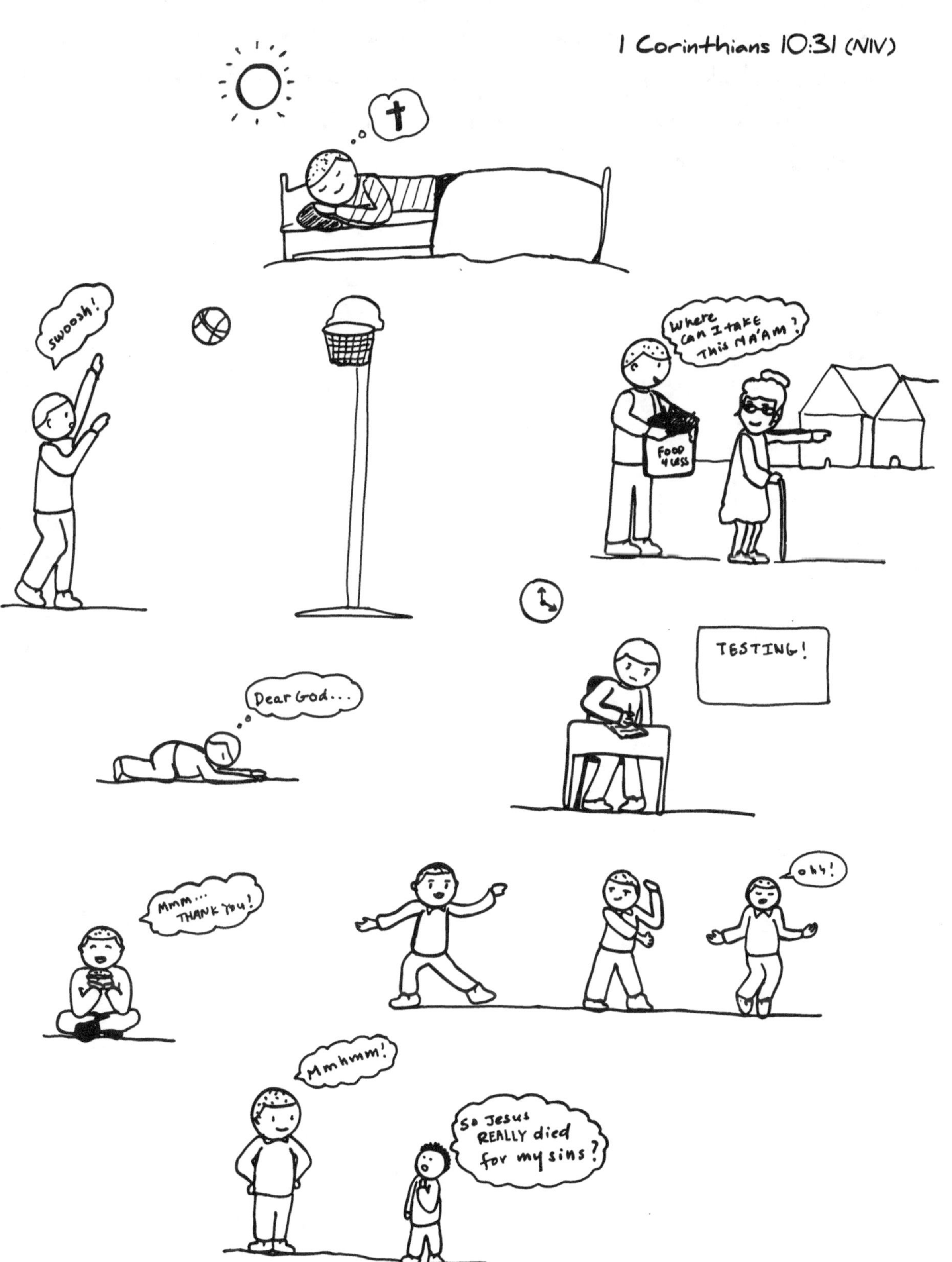

Everything that we do in life matters. It could even be a simple act such as helping a friend or resting at home. If we are by ourselves, we should be mindful that what we do should honor God. And if we are with others, we should do things in a way that can point them to God.

What are ways you can glorify God with the daily things you do?

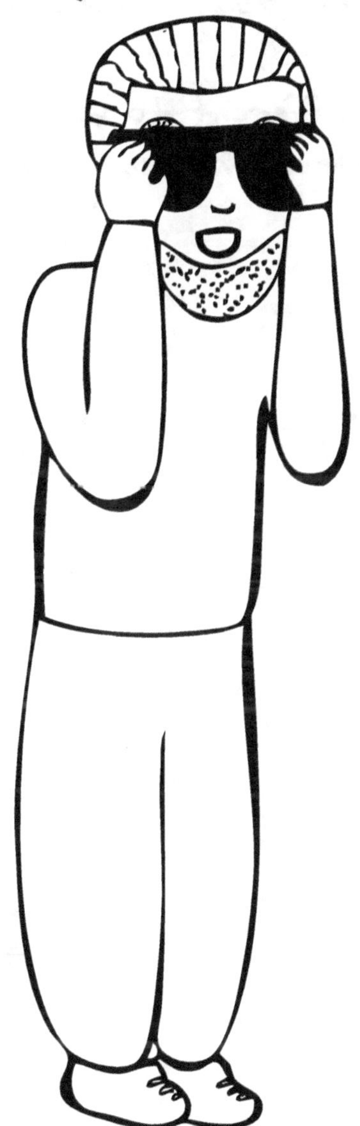

Wow, I once was blind
but now I can see!

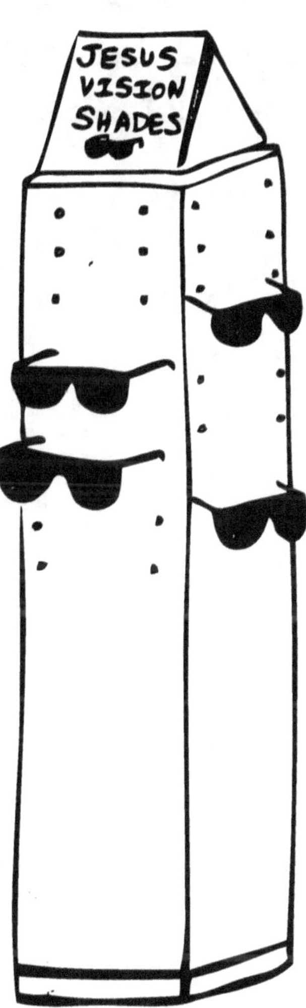

JESUS
VISION
SHADES

When we accept Jesus into our lives, it's almost like we have a new set of eyes. Things in our lives become more clear because we start to see things in this world as they really are. With new eyes, we'll know what to turn away from and what to go after. Sometimes our vision will get blurry if we let things of this world block our view. That's why it's important to turn to God's word and His spirit for a check up.

Has anything appeared different to you since you accepted Jesus? Draw or write down how it appeared before and after.

"The Lord is my chosen portion and my cup; you hold my lot."

Psalm 16:5

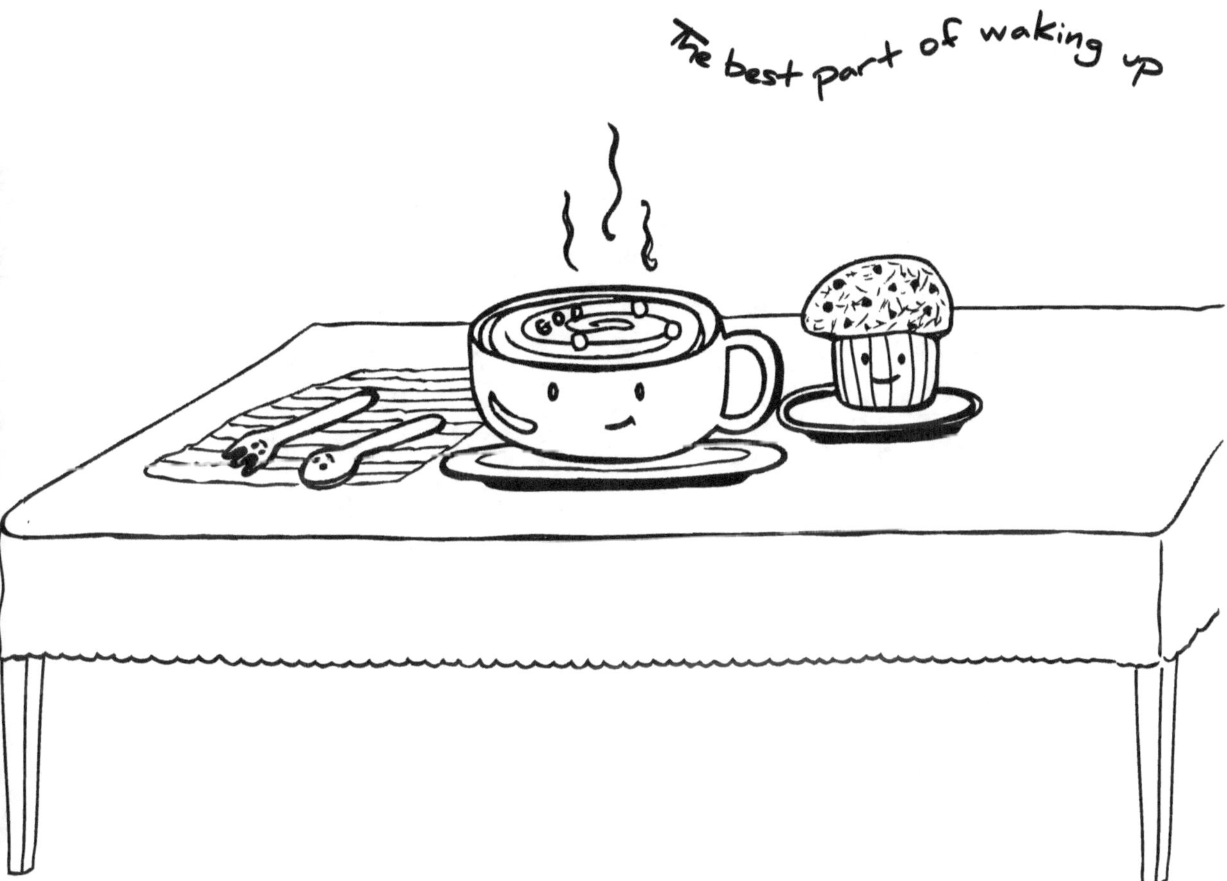

It's great to wake up knowing that God fills our cup with His spirit everyday and that we will never run dry. He gives each and every one of us exactly what we need at the exact time. Let Him be your everything and be happy for the portion He has given you today!

If your life is a cup, what does it look like? What is it filled with?

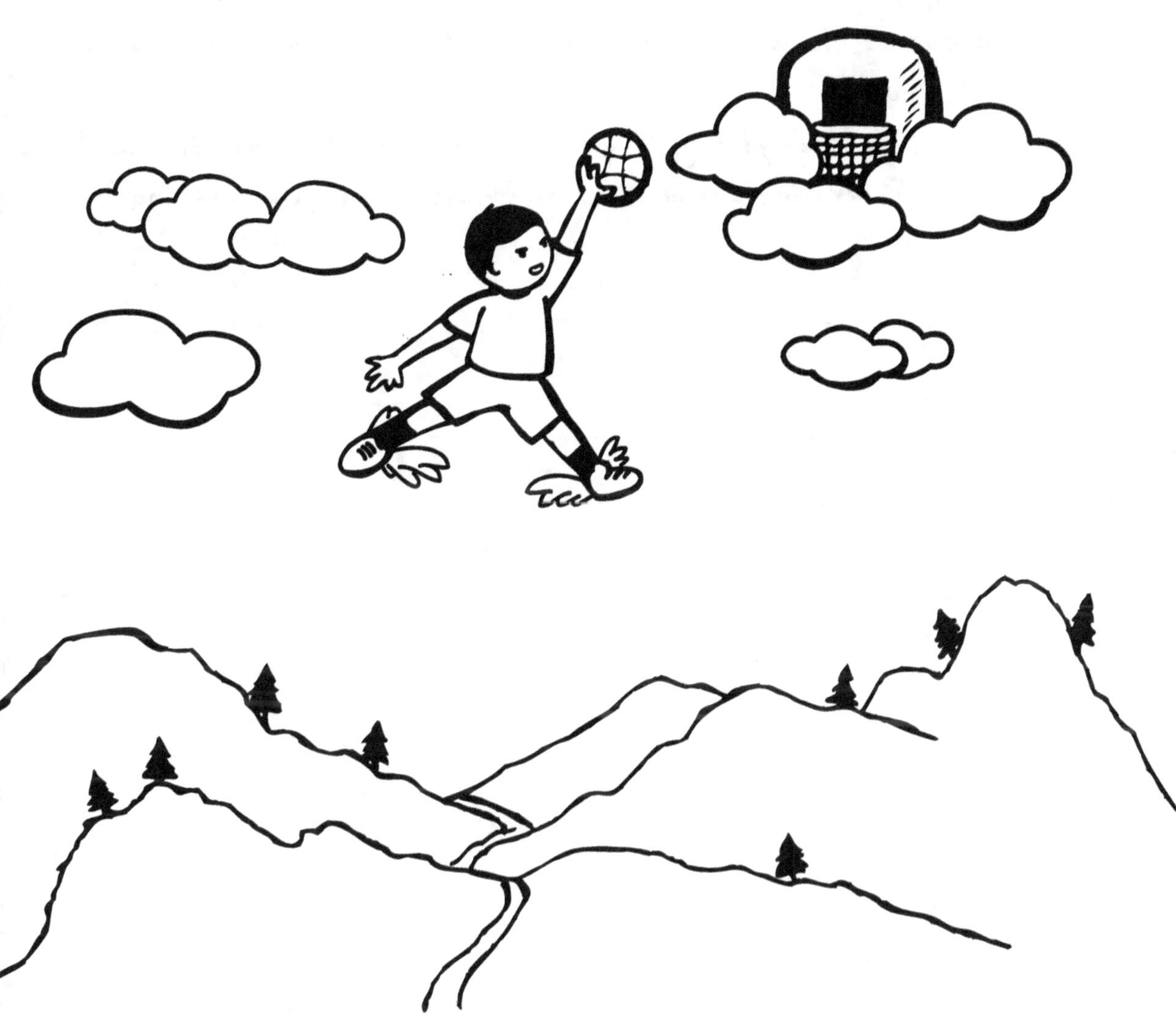

"They who wait for the LORD shall renew their strength; they shall mount up with wings like eagles; they shall run and not be weary; they shall walk and not faint."

Isaiah 40:31

#WINNING

Waiting can sometimes be one of the hardest things to do, whether it's for a person, an answer, or to do something you've always wanted. If what you ask God for doesn't happen right away, don't lose hope! God isn't ignoring us as we wait, but He is strengthening us and building our trust in Him. Wait on Him, and when the right time comes He will give you wings like eagles to achieve His goal for you!

Is there anything in your life that you find difficult to wait for? What do you do in those times of waiting?

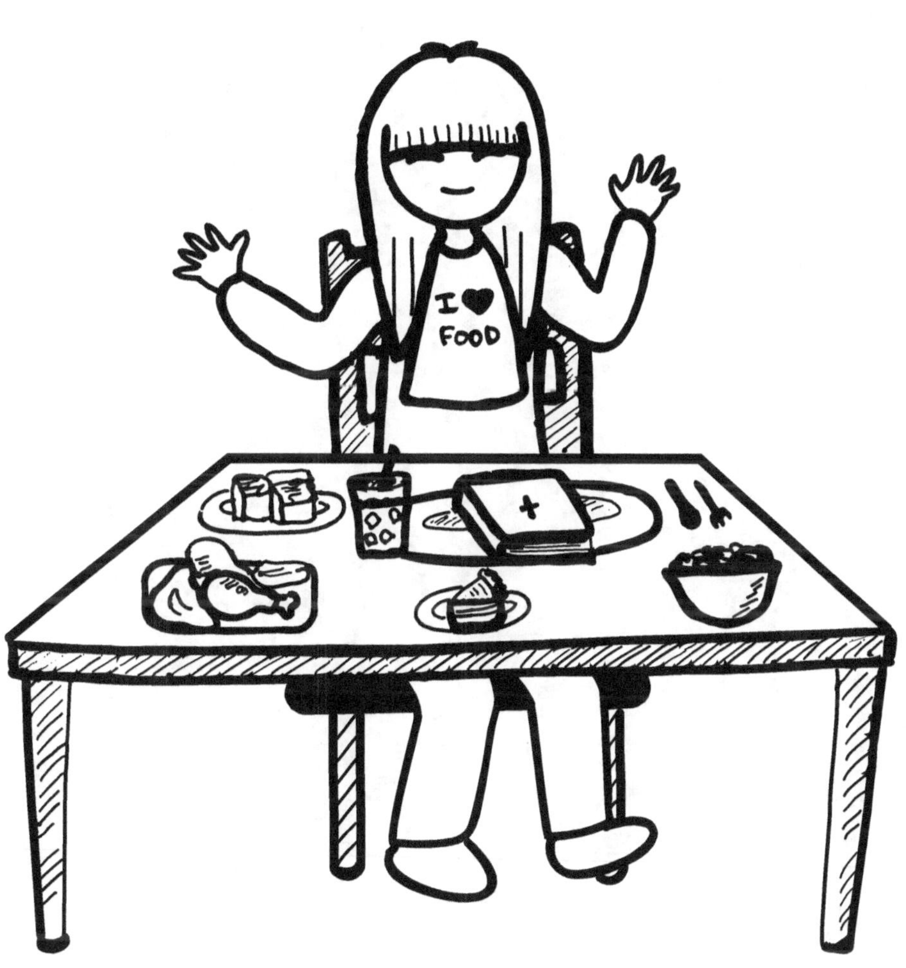

yum!
now this is what I call
Soul Food
I ♥ FOOD

    The best meal we can feed our soul is found in God's word. His promises and commandments will satisfy our every craving and have us keep wanting more. And the more we have of it, the stronger we will grow!

    What has your soul been craving? Do you turn to God's word to satisfy that craving or do you turn to other things?

"I have been crucified with Christ. It is no longer I who live, but Christ who lives in me. And the life I now live in the flesh I live by faith in the Son of God, who loved me and gave himself for me."

Galatians 2:20

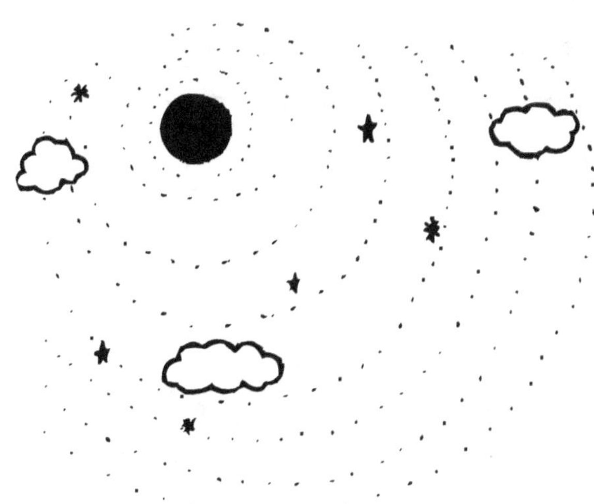

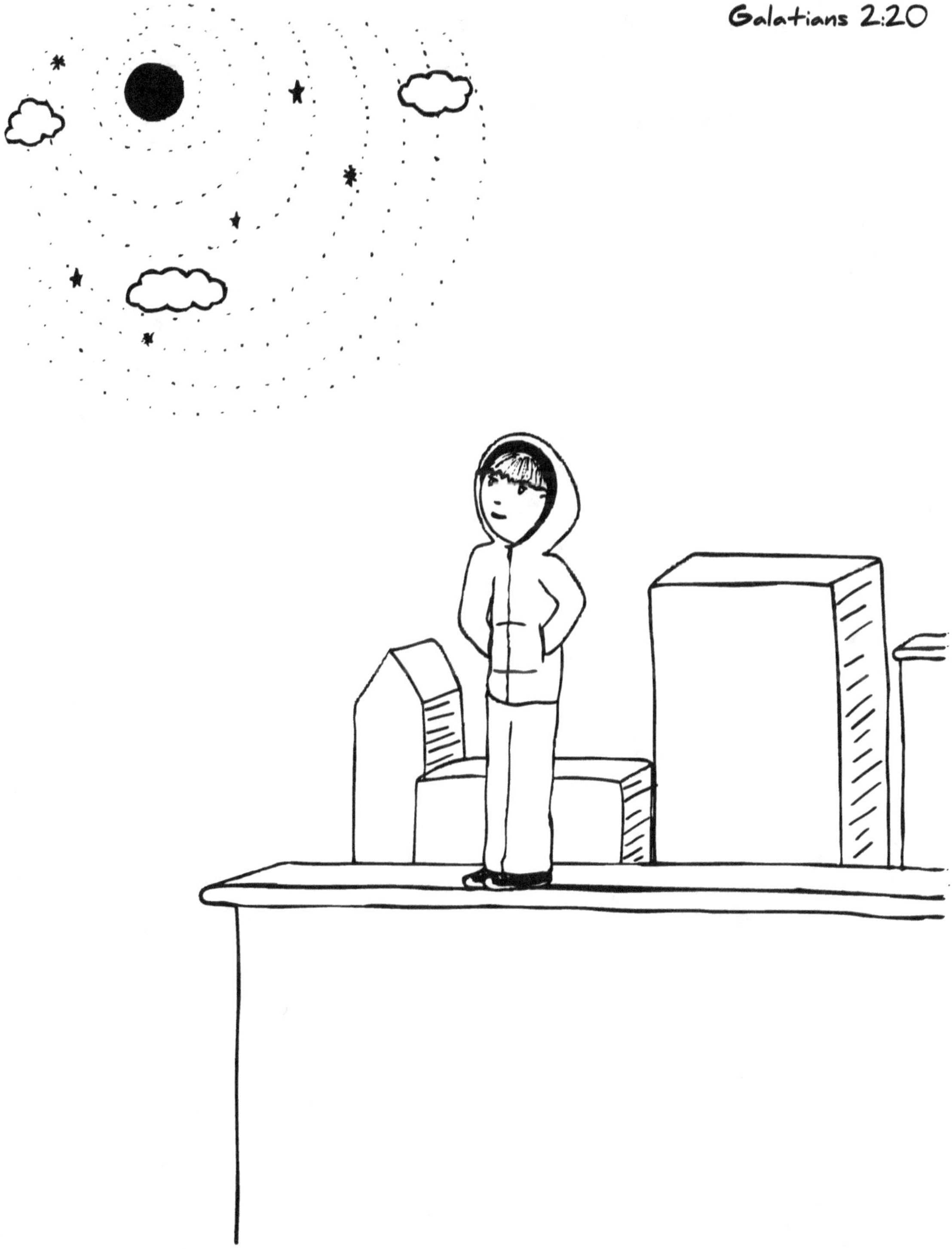

Sometimes we need to take a moment to remember that this life is not our own. When Jesus died on the cross for us, so did the selfish ways of our past. This means that our lives are not motivated by our own desires, but by the love of Jesus.

Think of the things that you spend most of your time doing. Are those things motivated by Jesus or are they motivated by something else?

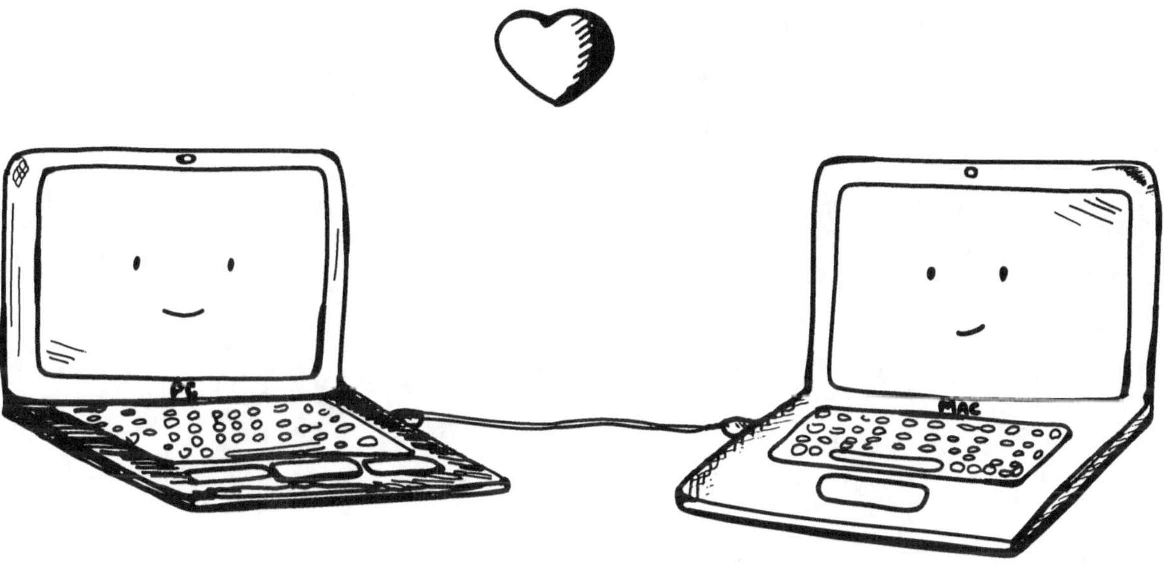

#LOVE YOUR ENEMIES

It feels natural to want to mistreat those who mistreat us. However, God wants us to act in a way that is against our human nature. Instead of getting back at our enemies, He tells us to love them by lending to them and treating them with kindness. We may not get the response we like, but God sees everything we do and He takes delight in our actions!

Has anyone mistreated you before? What did you do in that situation?

"For I know the plans I have for you," declares the Lord, "plans to prosper you and not to harm you, plans to give you hope and a future."

Jeremiah 29:11

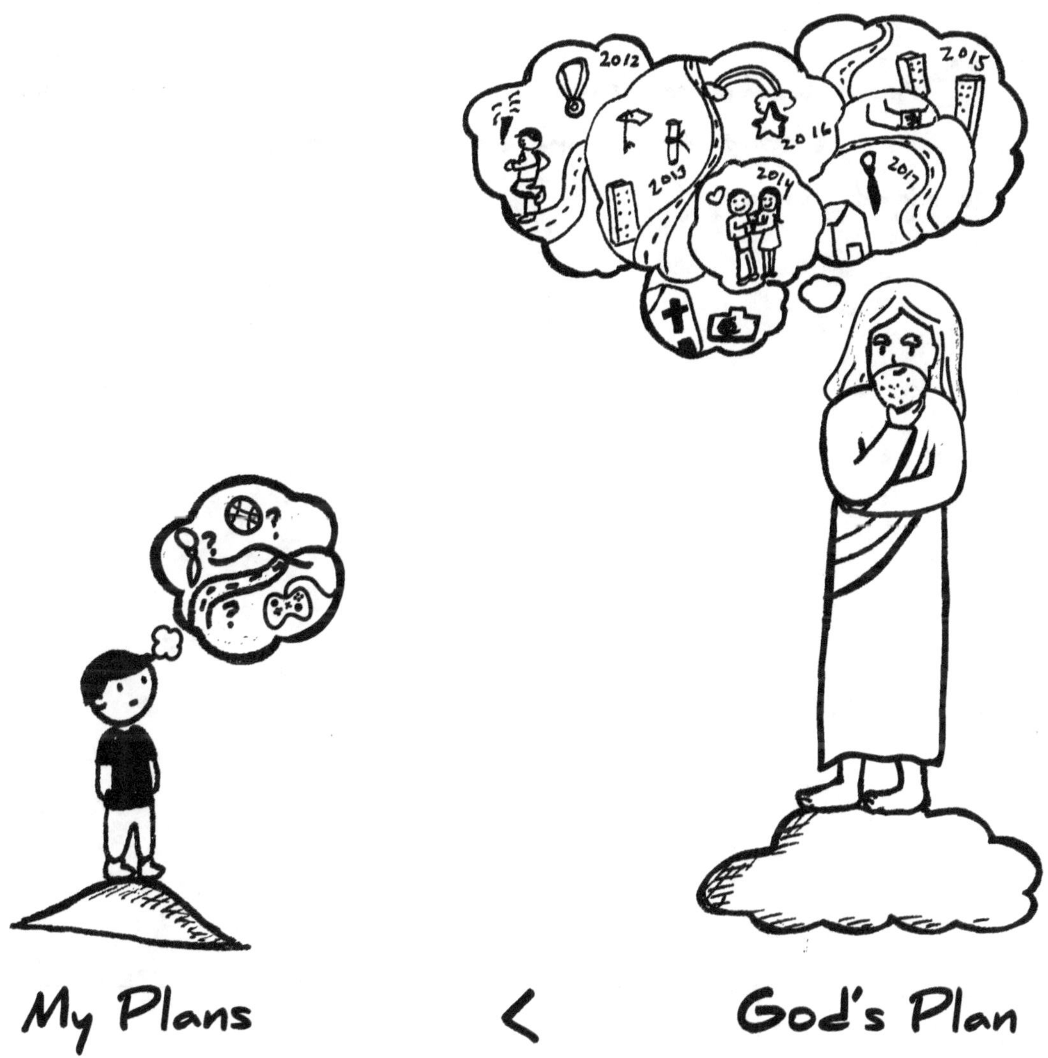

My Plans < God's Plan

Oftentimes we don't know what our future holds, whether it's what we will do tomorrow or in five years. The great thing is that God has already created a plan for us, and His plan is something greater than what we can ever imagine! It's still important to make plans, but know that God is the one who controls where those plans go.

Draw or write down some plans you have for this year. Pray about them and ask God to direct them to the right place.

"Take captive every thought to make it obedient to Christ "

2 Corinthians 10:5

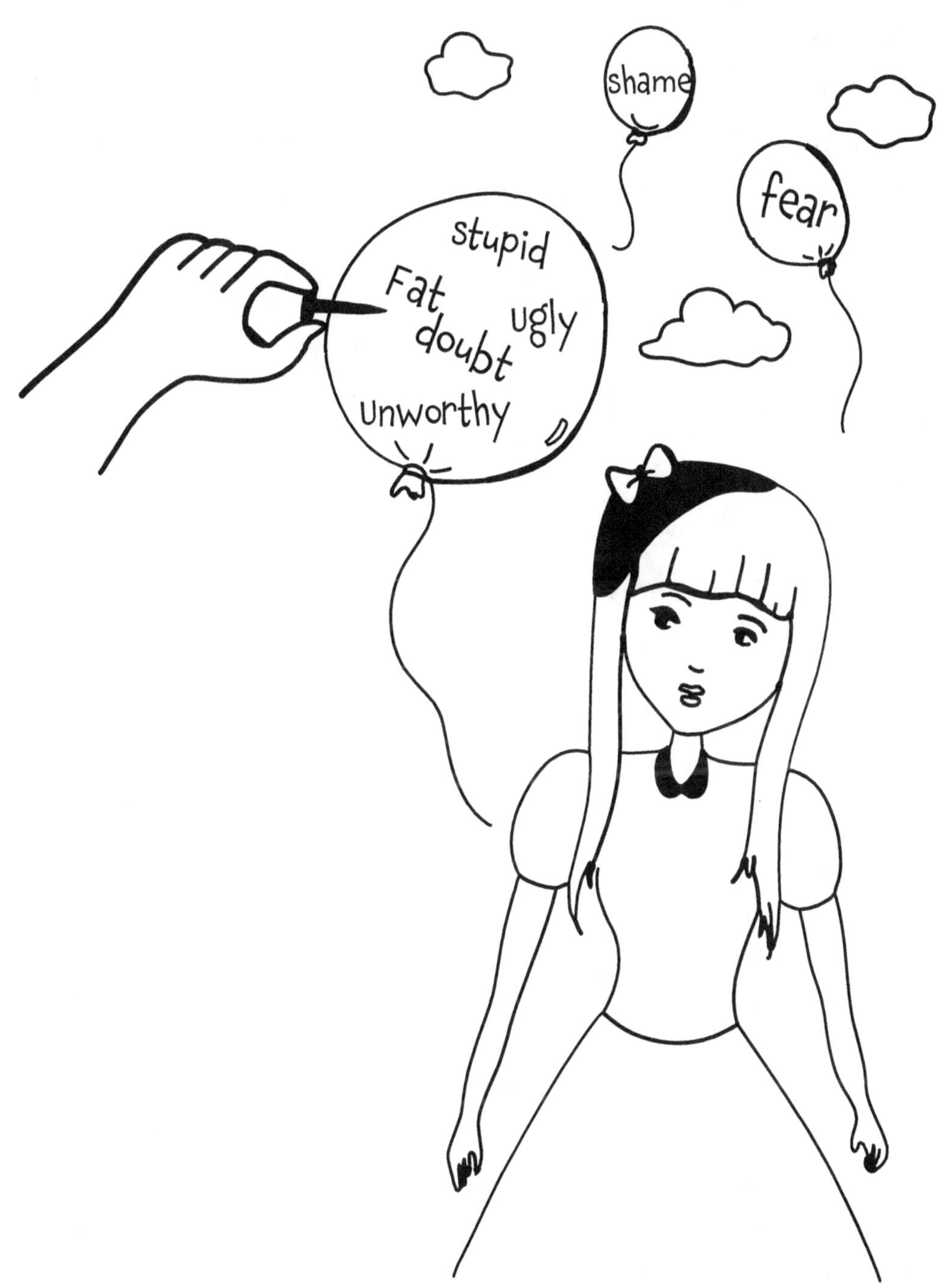

There will be days when we think negatively about ourselves and let our mind control our actions. However, in those times we must fight those thoughts with the truth of God's word. He tell us that we are fearfully and wonderfully made, so don't ever think you are anything less than that!

Do you find yourself stuck on a certain thought that gets you down? What are some bible verses that can knock out those thoughts?

"Finally, brothers, whatever is true, whatever is honorable,
whatever is just, whatever is pure, whatever is lovely,
whatever is commendable, if there is any excellence, if there
is anything worthy of praise, think about these things."

Philippians 4:8

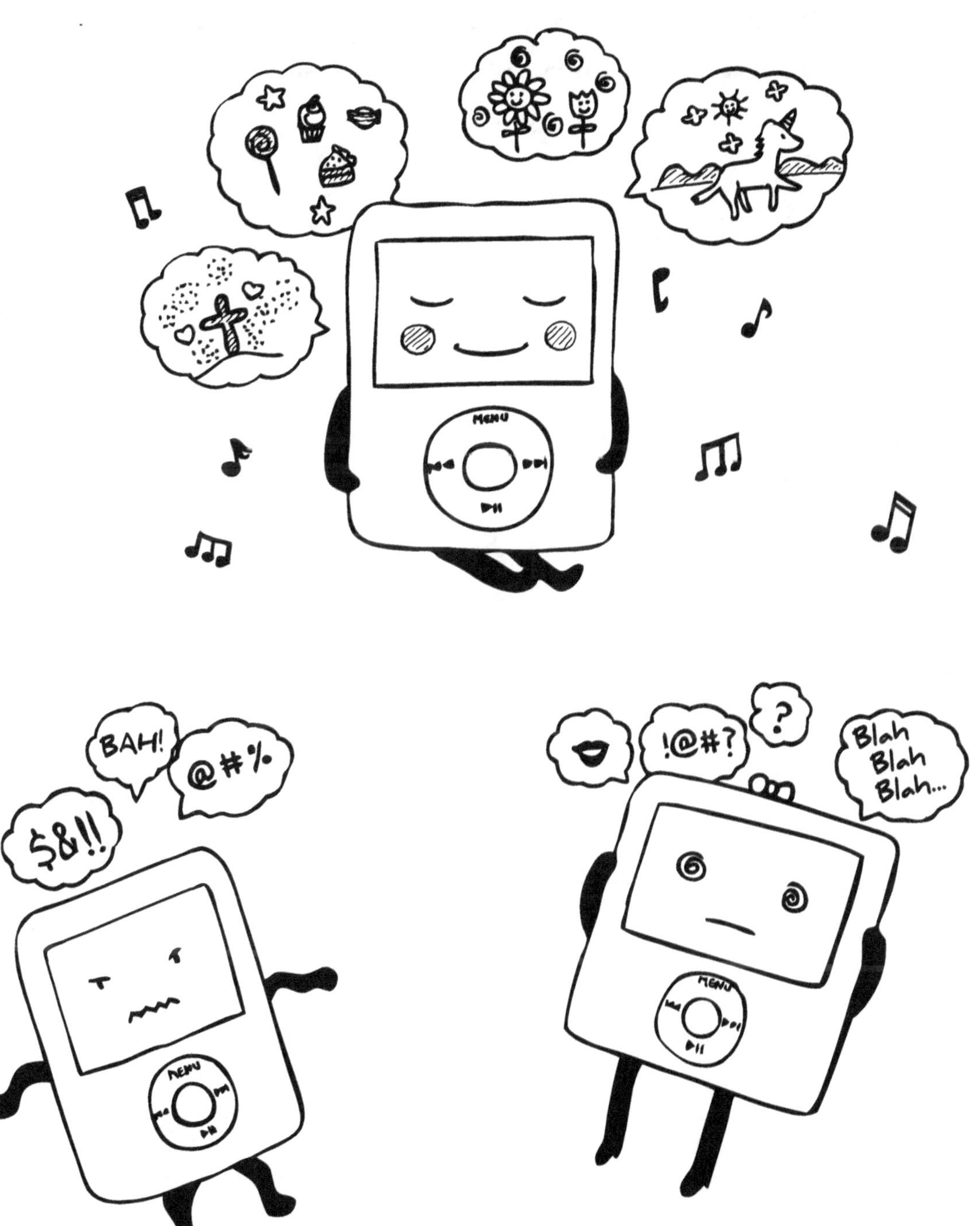

If we want to have our minds and hearts set on God, it means choosing carefully what we watch and listen to. For some of us, music can affect the way we think and act. That is why it's important to know what the songs we listen to are actually about.

What songs do you listen to and what do they make you think about? Do they make you think about things that God says He wants us to think about?

"Therefore, if anyone is in Christ, he is a new creation. The old has passed away; behold, the new has come."

2 Corinthians 5:17

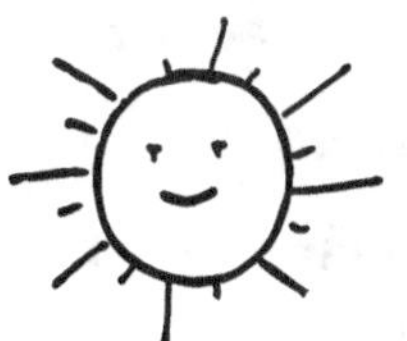

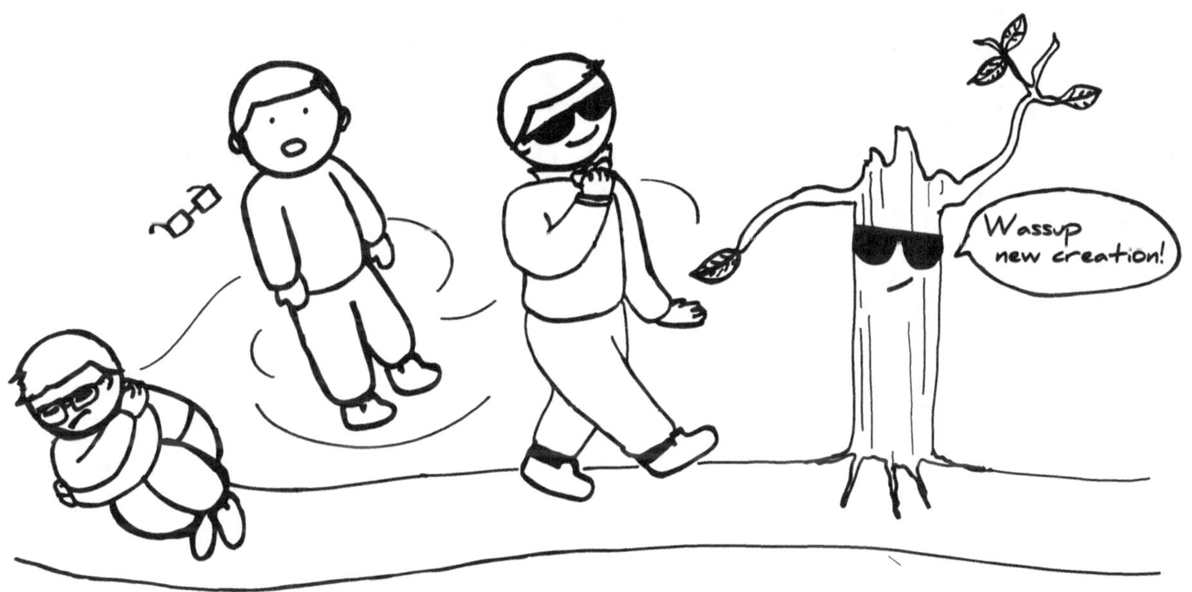

Being a new creation means that you are completely transformed from the inside out. Even our bad habits and thoughts can be replaced with new things that God delights in. There might be days we mess up, but know that God continues to work in us even through our messiness. Be confident in Him because He is doing a great work in you!

What are some things God has made new in your life? Draw or write down a before and after picture.

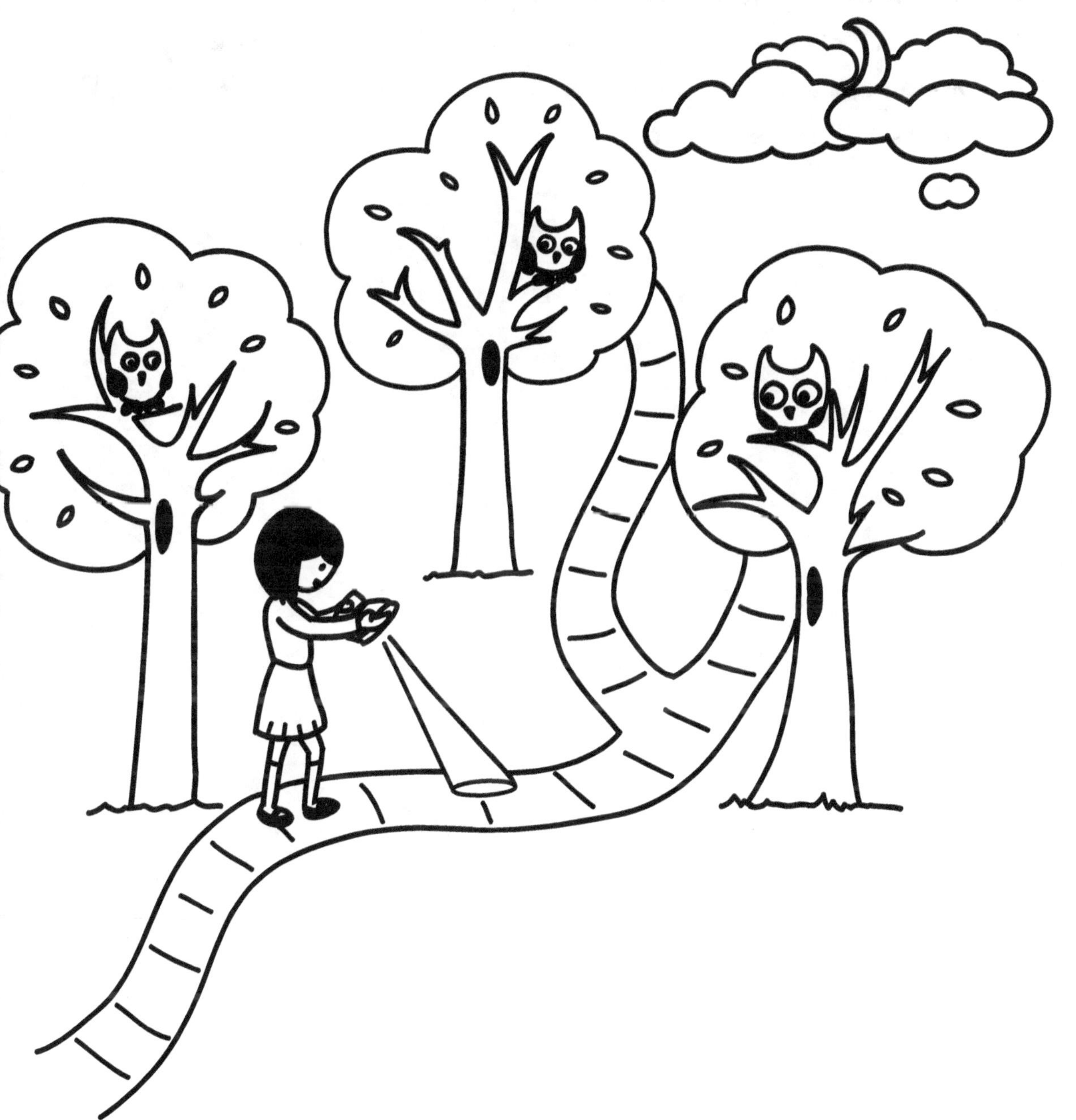

"Your word is a lamp for my feet,
a light on my path"

Psalm 119:105

There are so many directions we can go in life. Without the right guide, it would be like walking in the dark. Good thing God gives us His word to help guide us! Use this guide as much as you can in life and you will be sure to walk in the right direction.

Write down a verse below that has guided you in making a decision. Draw or write down the outcome of following that verse.

"For everything there is a season, and a time for every matter under heaven"

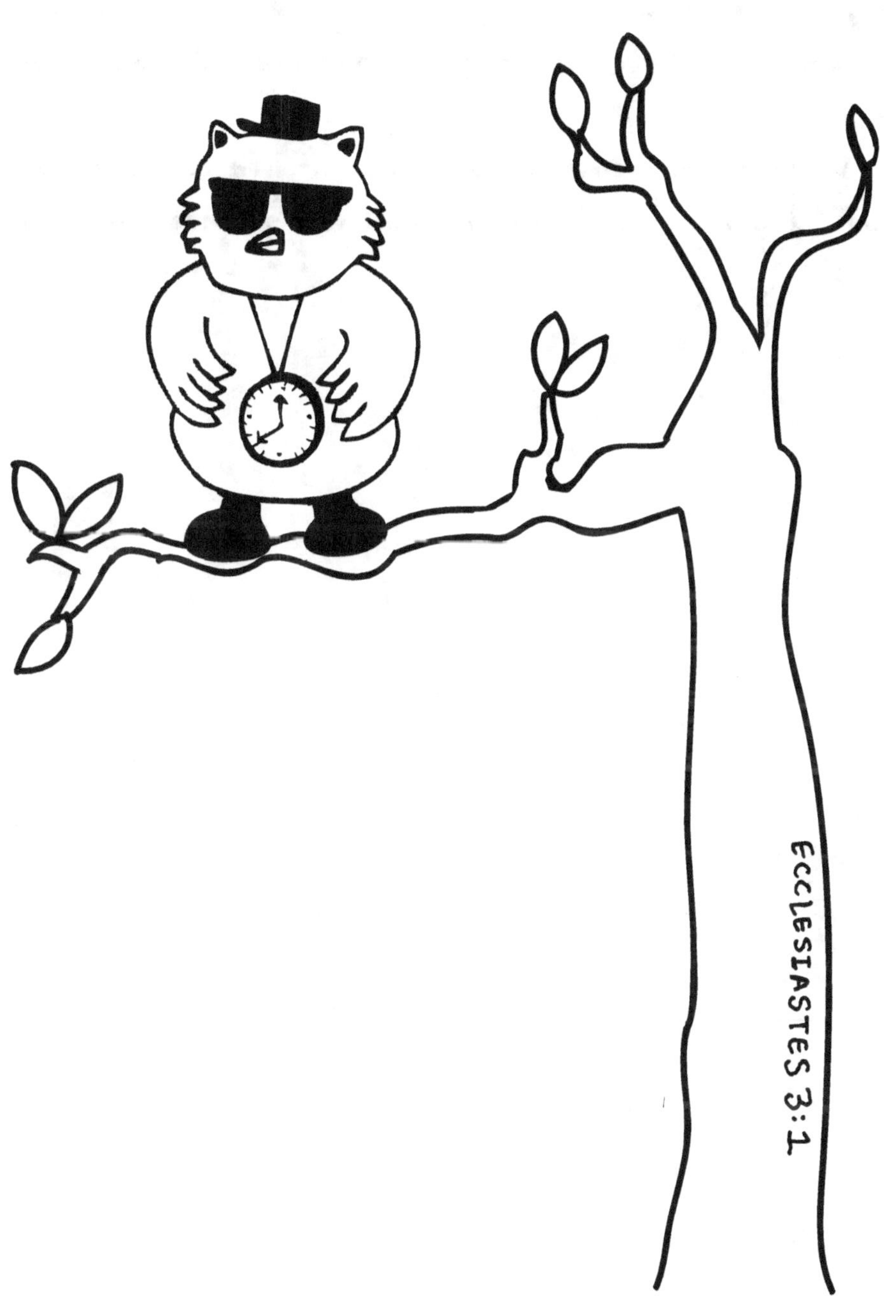

Sometimes we want to know why things happen or when things will happen, so we try to understand and do more than what is asked of us. It's not a bad thing to wonder, but keep in mind that we cannot control or know the reason for every event in our life. This will surely stress us out! Know that God's timing is perfect. He wants us to trust Him in whatever situation we are in.

What are some events in your life you are unsure about? How can you trust God with these events?

"For you formed my inward parts; you knitted me together in my mother's womb."

Psalm 139:13

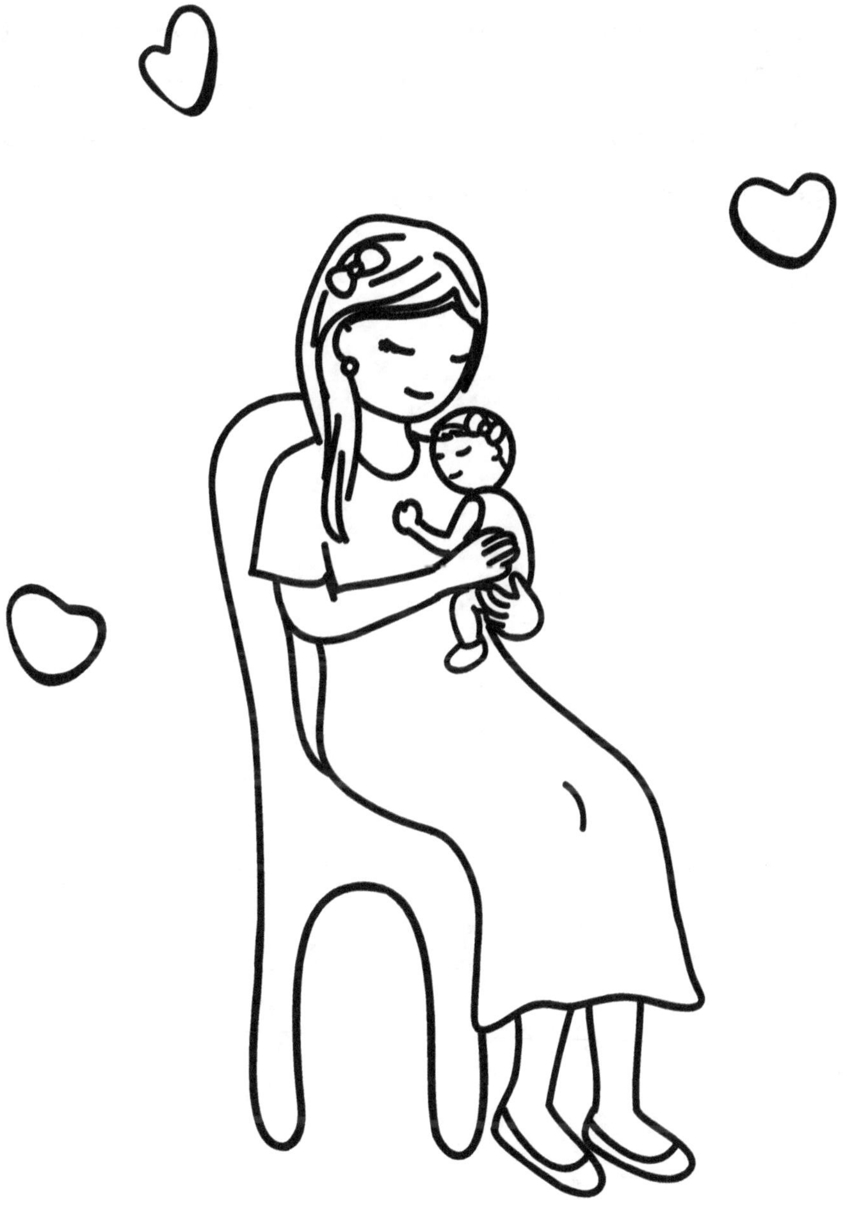

God knew exactly what He was doing when He made you. He thought of you even before you were born and carefully crafted every part of your body for a beautiful purpose. The way you are right now is a a masterpiece of His creation!

Do you appreciate the parts of your body? Draw a picture frame below and then draw yourself inside that frame. Tell yourself that you are a work of art and that there is no one created like you!

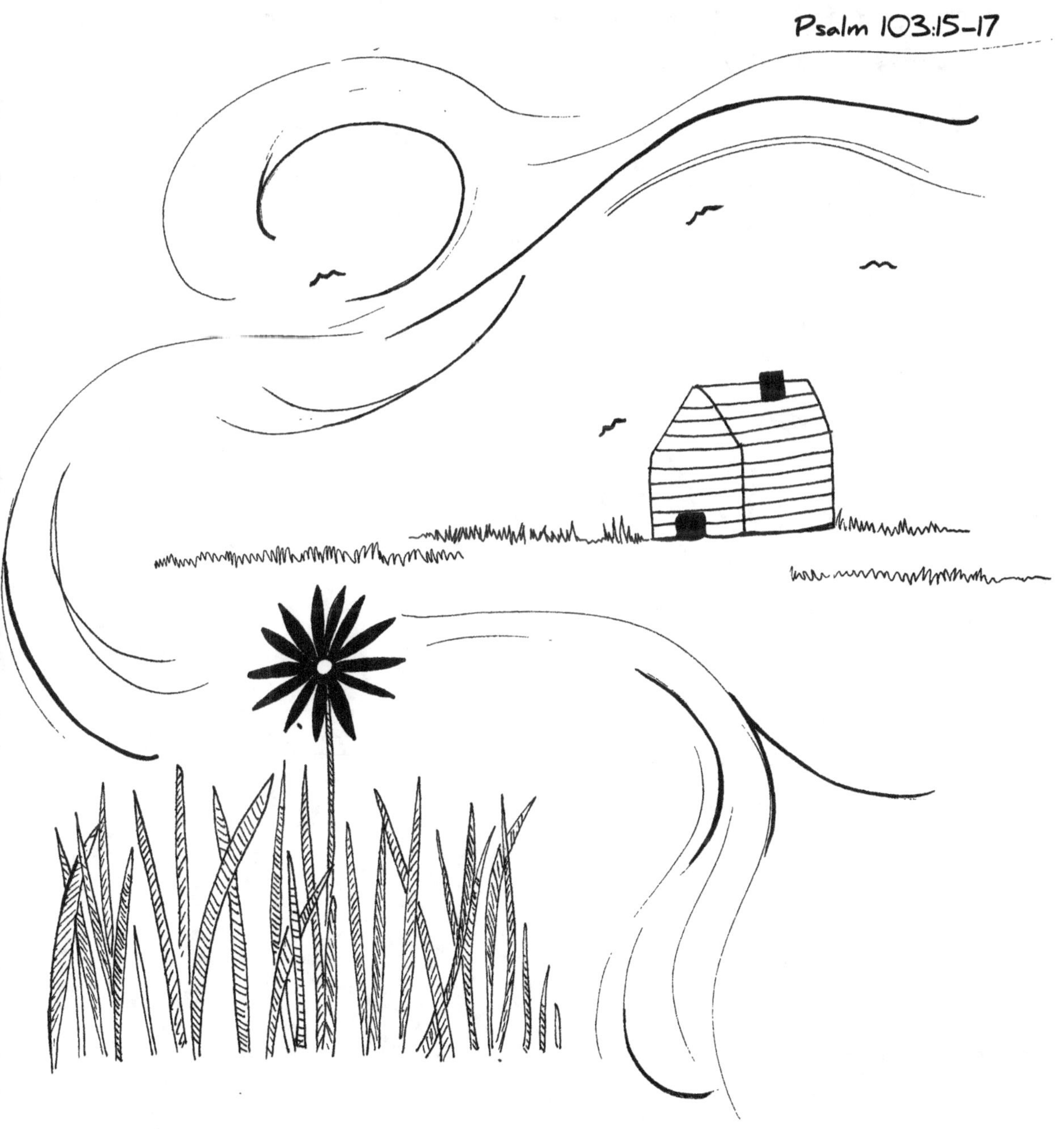

"As for man, his days are like grass;
he flourishes like a flower of the field;
for the wind passes over it, and it is
gone, and its place knows it no more."

"But the steadfast love of the Lord
is from everlasting to everlasting
on those who fear him, and his
righteousness to children's children"

Psalm 103:15-17

The things we have in this world won't last forever. For example, the toys that you have, the house that you live in, even the people you love will go away one day. But one thing that remains forever is God. He never stops loving us! If we put our trust in Him, our spirit too will live on forever. And if we live our lives for Him, what we do too will last forever.

Do you want an everlasting life? Do you want to do things that make a lasting impact? Draw or write down your ideas below.

"Welcome one another as Christ has welcomed you, for the glory of God."

Romans 15:7

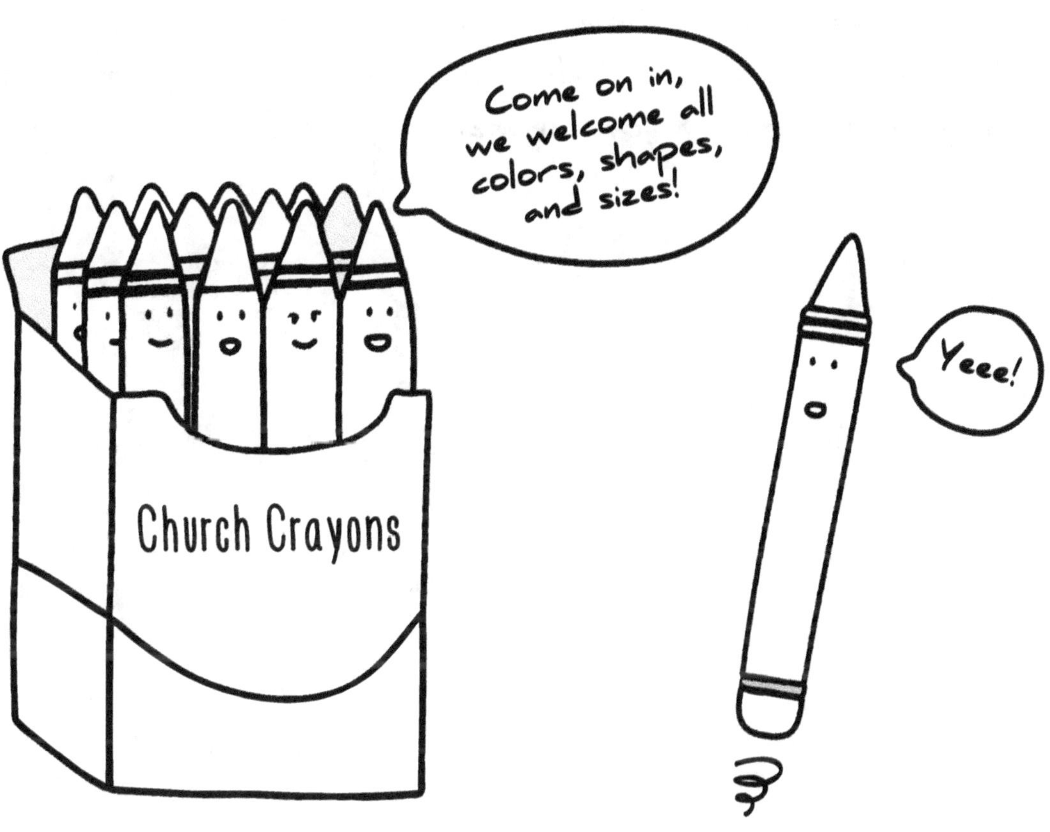
Come on in, we welcome all colors, shapes, and sizes!
Church Crayons
Yeee!

In the family of God, everyone should be accepted no matter what they look like, where they come from, or who they are. God doesn't separate us depending on our color and background, so we shouldn't separate ourselves from others either. Let's greet one another with love and compassion because we are all members of one big family!

Was there a time you felt welcomed in a new place? How did it make you feel? How can you make others feel more welcomed at your church or home?

"He Himself bore our sins in His body on the cross, so that we might die to sin and live to righteousness; for by His wounds you were healed."

1 Peter 2:24 (NASB)

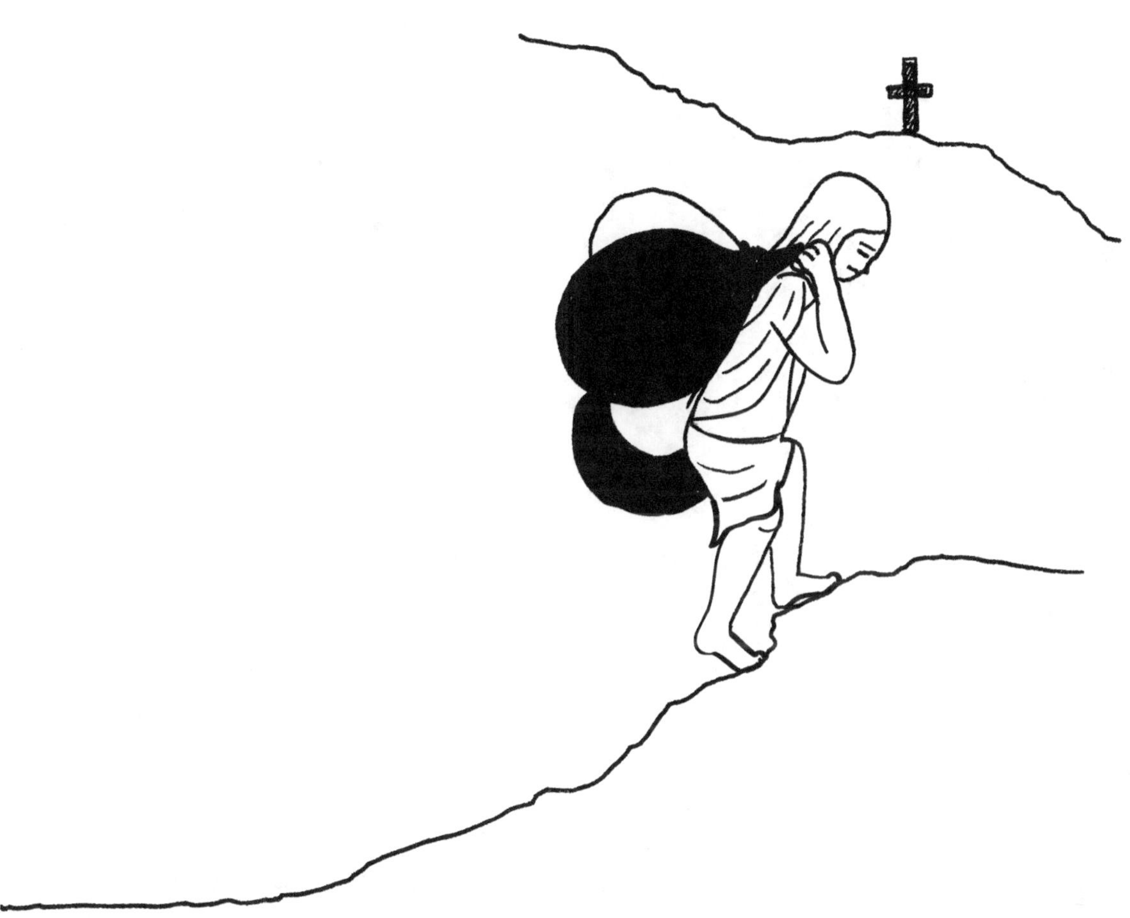

Jesus carried the weight of our sin all the way to the cross. Though it was painful, He did it because He loves us. He loves us so much that He even died on the cross so that our sins would die with Him.

No sin is too much for Him to carry. Is there anything you want Him to carry for you?

"The Lord is my rock, my fortress and my deliverer, my God, my rock, in whom I take refuge"

Psalm 18:2

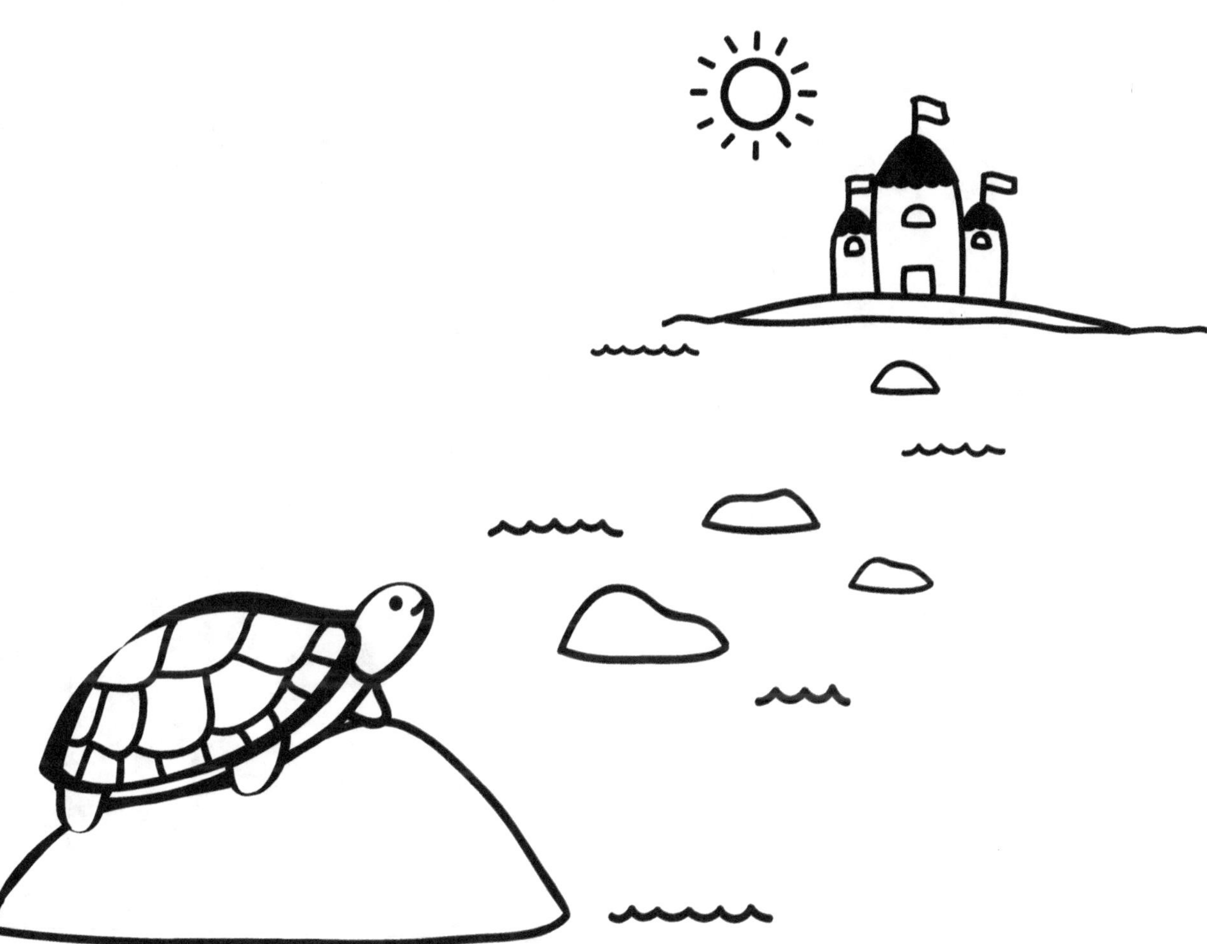

When you feel like you are in deep water and there is no way of getting out, call on God. He will lift you up because your faith is grounded in Him. Keep your head up and trust that God will deliver you to a place of safety and peace. He provides for each step of the way!

Draw or write about a place you are afraid of. Now put God in that place. How does He protect you in that place?

"It is more blessed to give than to receive."

Acts 20:35

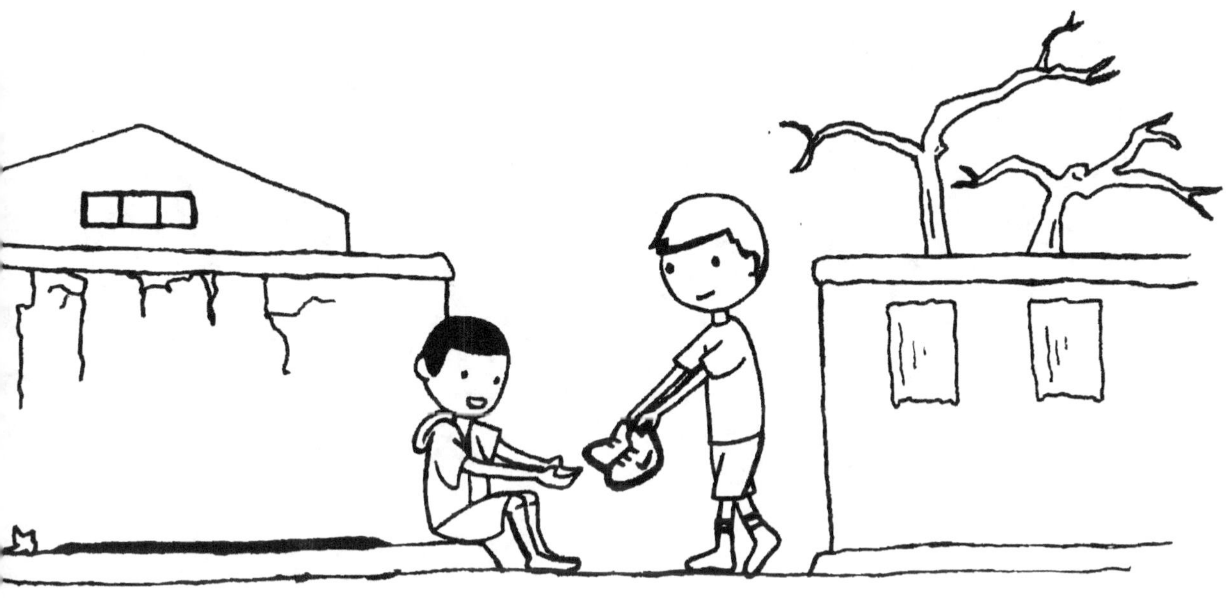

It feels great to receive things from others, but as a child of God it should feel even better to give things. What we give to others doesn't just have to be money or presents. It can also be our time, prayer, and talents! Whatever you give, give with a heart of thankfulness for the many things God has given to you.

Was there a time you gave someone something that meant a lot to you? How did that person react? How did it make you feel?

"Watch and pray that you may not enter
into temptation. The spirit indeed is willing, but
the flesh is weak."

Matthew 26:41

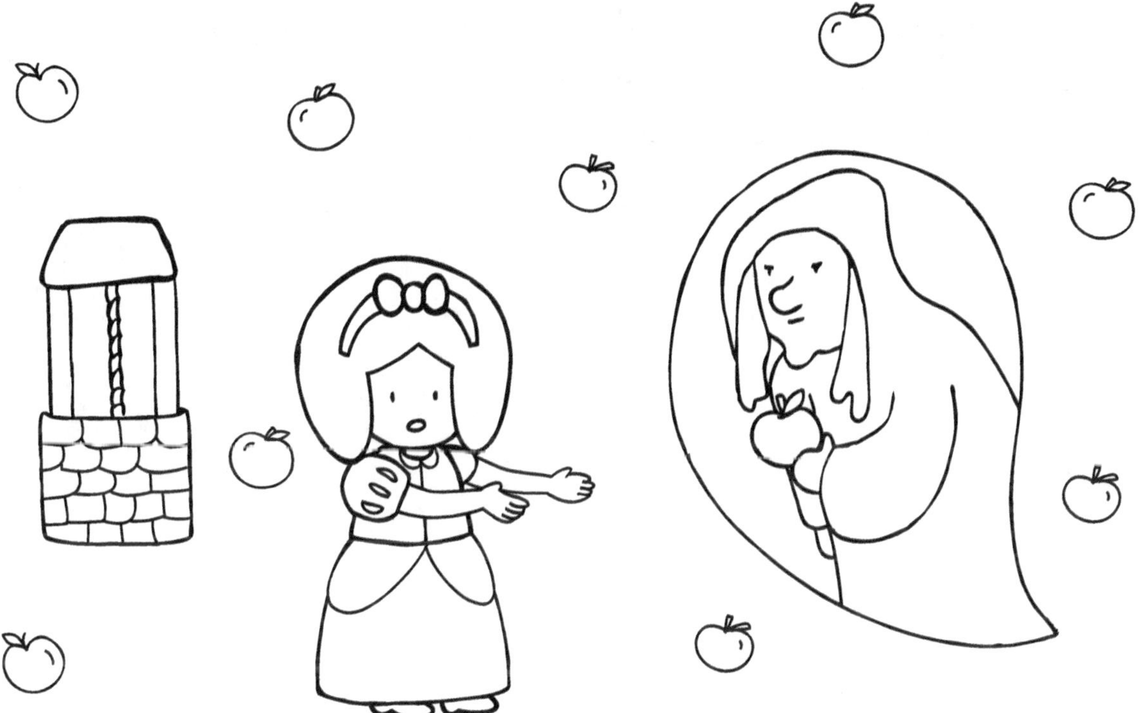

Flee from temptation

Sometimes we get into situations where it's easy to want to do the wrong thing, especially if that thing looks and feels good. This is why Jesus tells us to wake up our mind and pray in situations we know we have a lack of control in. Don't believe that you have to give in to temptations. Believe that Jesus will protect you and help you flee from them!

Have you ever faced a situation where you know something you want is wrong but you still can't help but want it? What did you do?

"Do not be conformed to this world, but be transformed
by the renewal of your mind."
Romans 12:2

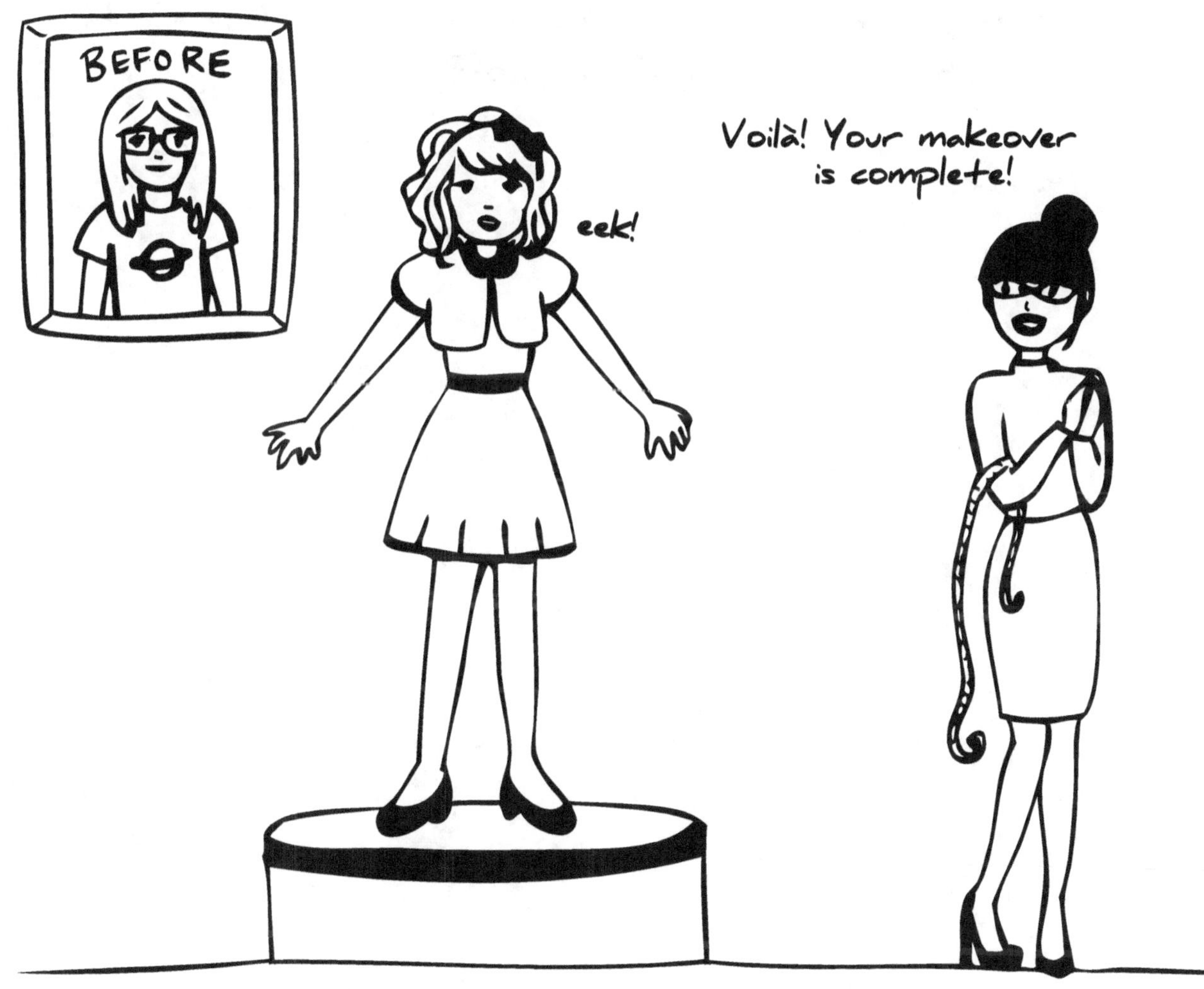

BEFORE
eek!
Voilà! Your makeover
is complete!

To be transformed doesn't mean we change our outer appearance. A transformation happens when we become a completely new person from the inside out. This means there is a change in our heart, the way we think, and the way we act. It is only by God's grace we can be changed. Don't feel pressured to change for others, but stay true to who God calls you to be!

Have you noticed any changes in the way you think and act as you have gotten to know God more? How would you illustrate your transformation?

"I have no greater joy than to hear that my children are walking in the truth."

3 John 1:4

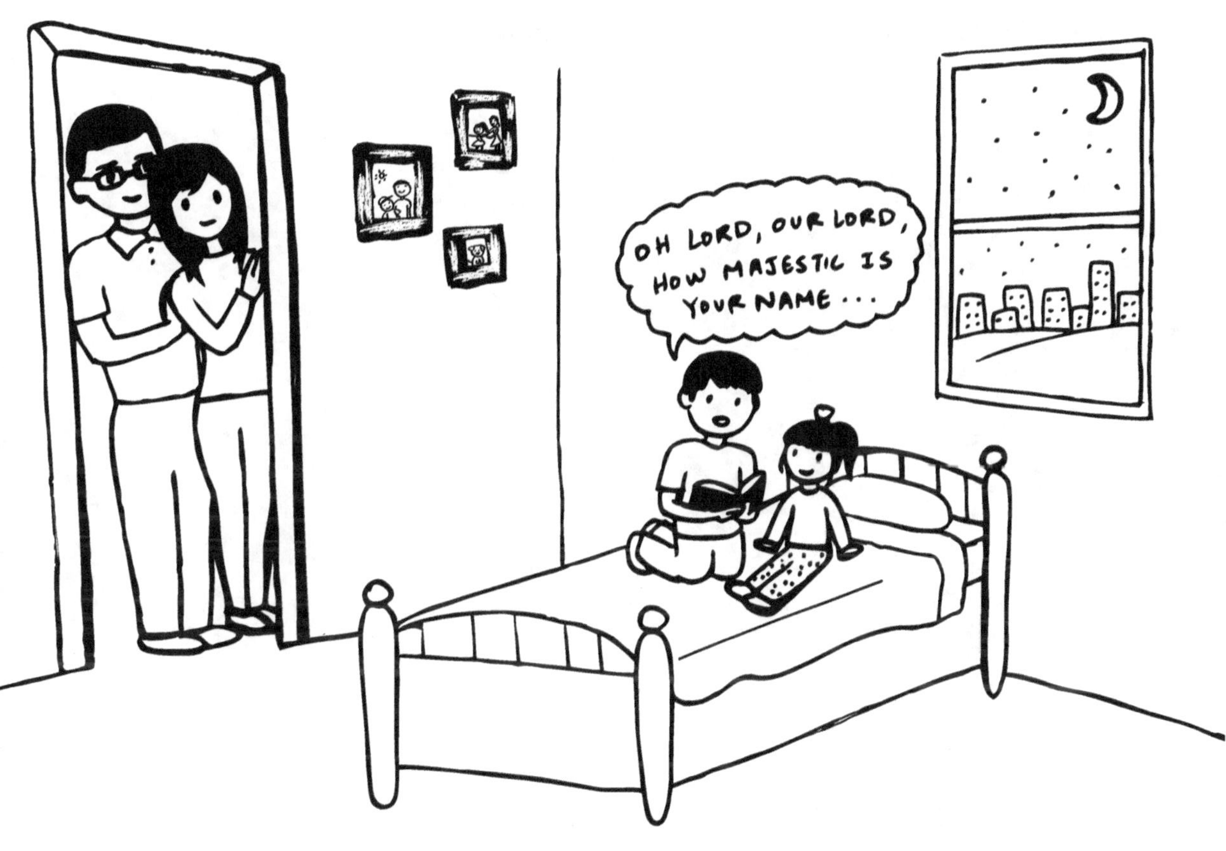

There are a lot of things we can do to make our parents proud of us. But what makes them most proud is our devotion to God. The best is when we are doing the things God wants us to do such as praying and reading His word without being told to. What matters most is that we do these things because we want to know God more!

What motivates you to walk in God's truth? Draw or write those things down below.

"I thank my God in all my remembrance of you,
always in every prayer of mine for you all making my
prayer with joy, because of your partnership in the
gospel from the first day until now."

Philippians 1:3-5

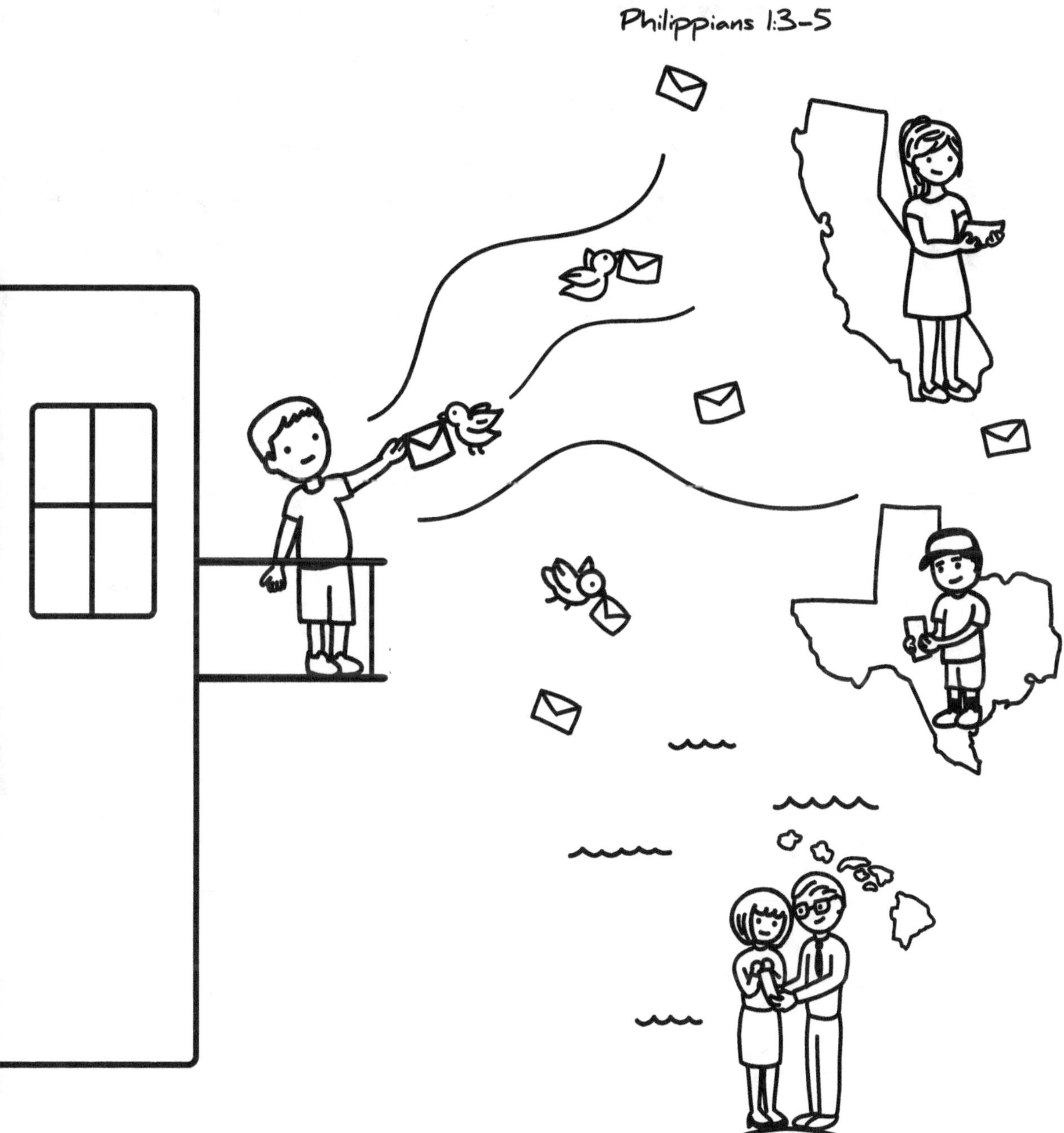

It's a blessing that God calls us to be set apart from the world. It's an even bigger blessing that He surrounds us with people who will walk alongside us. Though they may not be with us in person, they are there with us in spirit, always praying, always believing. Sometimes we need that encouragement to help us get through the day!

Are there people in your life who have helped you in your walk with God? Take time right now to pray for them and thank God for their care in your life. Write them a letter or draw them a picture as an expression of your thanks.